TIM BOWLER

SHADOWS

Cornelsen

Tim Bowler
Shadows

Herausgegeben von
Gunthild Porteous-Schwier, Ingrid Ross

Verlagsredaktion
Neil Porter

Technische Umsetzung
Gisela Hoffmann

Umschlagillustrationen
Corel Library; William R. Sallaz/Image Bank

This edition of *Shadows* is published by agreement with Oxford University Press.

Herausgeber der *Cornelsen Senior English Library:*
Prof. Dr. Albert-Reiner Glaap

www.cornelsen.de

1. Auflage, 3. Druck 2007 / 06

Alle Drucke dieser Auflage sind inhaltlich unverändert und können im Unterricht nebeneinander verwendet werden.

Druck: CS-Druck CornelsenStürtz, Berlin

ISBN 978-3-464-37159-6

Inhalt gedruckt auf säurefreiem Papier aus nachhaltiger Forstwirtschaft.

CONTENTS

= Person

= important details

= vocabulary

Abbreviations

adj	adjective	jdm./jdn.	jemandem/en
derog	derogatory	n	noun
e.g.	exempli gratia; for example	pl	plural
esp.	especially	sb.	somebody
etc.	et cetera; and so on	sl	slang
fml	formal	sth.	something
i.e.	id est; in other words	usu.	usually
infml	informal	v	verb

All pronunciations given are British English.
Words relating to the game of squash are not explained at the bottom of the page on which they occur. You can find them instead in the 'The Game of Squash' on pp. 175–177.

ONE

Jamie tried to ignore the shouts from the spectators, the urging, the willing, the madness. Across the squash court, Danny glared back at him. But there was an element of triumph in the boy's face. His cockiness was gone – the first two games had at least wiped that from him – but having fought back with characteristic aggression to two games all, he clearly felt he was in with a chance of taking the match.

Jamie tried to focus his mind and energy. He knew the pressure was on him now. He had had a two – love lead and thrown it away. He had never beaten Danny in the twelve months since the boy had moved down from the north, and though this was meant to be a minor affair, the semi-final of the Under 19 Knockout in the 'friendly' atmosphere of their own club, it was obvious that everyone saw it as a taster for the Regional Championships in two weeks' time.

He glanced up at the faces in the gallery. They were all there: Andy, Joe, the bar crowd, and, of course, Bob Powell blustering on with pride every time Danny won a rally, as though his son were a god and not the arrogant poser that he was. But there was only one face up there Jamie was bothered about. And right now he did not dare to look at it.

▷ **1** *urging:* (here) act of encouraging sb. strongly **2** *willing:* strong desire for sb. to win · *glare back at sb.:* stare at sb. who is staring at you **4** *cockiness* (infml): overconfidence **6** *be in with a chance:* still have a chance **11** *Under 19 Knockout:* competition for players younger than 19 in which the winning player at each stage competes in the next stage and the losing one no longer takes part **12** *taster* (here): Vorgeschmack **14** *gallery:* spectator seats above or behind the court **15** *bluster on:* speak loudly and aggressively **17** *poser* ['pəʊzə]: show-off

'Fifth and final game,' called Geoff. 'Love – all.'

The shouts from the gallery died away and he forced his mind back to the match. Danny walked over to the right service box, glanced his way for a second, and served.

A floater, hanging high. Jamie drove the ball down the backhand side wall and took up the T position mid-court. Danny powered it back across court, too close to the far wall for him to cut it off. He scuttled back and played a boast off the side wall, hoping the ball would catch the nick where the wall met the floor and give him an outright winner. But Danny scooped it up and played a cross-court drop.

Jamie dived forward. Earlier in the match he would have reached this one but now, with his energy almost spent, he stopped, knowing it was out of reach, anxious to save what strength he had left.

There was clapping from the gallery, then Powell's voice bellowed out.

'Good boy, Danny, good boy! He's finished!'

He heard disapproving noises from Joe who, as owner of the club, always tried to curb Powell's open hostility towards his son's opponents. It never did any good.

'One – love,' called Geoff.

The next serve came, another floater, higher this time and dropping close to the back wall. Somehow he managed to volley it before it dipped into the dead spot at the back of the court, but it was a poor return. He was out of position and Danny had already moved to the front of the court for the drop shot. Another simple point.

'Two – love,' called Geoff.

He was playing like a fool, giving away rallies like a beginner. He glanced back to the gallery and this time forced himself to look at the figure in the top right corner. The face was impassive, like hewn marble. There was no expression in the eyes. but the mouth was tight.

The next serve came, another curler, but not so close to the side wall this time. He struck out, aiming across court, but Danny cut it off and volleyed towards the backhand nick. He struggled to the front of the court and just managed to flick it back. It was meant to be a lob but it was too low. Danny leapt, drove it down the forehand side and buried it at the back of the court.

'That's the one!' shouted Powell. 'Kill him!'

He glared up and saw Joe trying to calm Powell again. But Powell had eyes for Danny alone. From the top right corner of the gallery there was only stillness.

'Three – love,' called Geoff.

He turned back to the court, determined to fight back but now desperately jaded. It seemed to him suddenly that he'd been on a squash court every waking moment of his sixteen years. And before the next service came, he just had time to reflect that this wasn't far from the truth. No wonder these walls had come to feel like a cell; and it was a cell of tension, tempered by moments of jubilation, but dominated for the most part by an ambition he sensed he would never fulfil.

The serve came, again a high curler. He struck out early, this time down the side wall, a better length than he had managed for a while but still short. Danny raced across and drove it the same way. Jamie followed suit and soon they were locked in a duel down the side wall, each aiming for the perfect width and the perfect length to make the ball cling to the side wall and die in the nick at the back.

Keep it tight, he told himself. Keep a good length. Keep plugging it down the side wall. Make him go for the risky winner.

And there it was. Danny had driven the ball in short, aiming for the forehand nick, but it was loose. Jamie reached it and played a drop to the same part of the court. Danny lunged and barged against him. The ball rolled along the floor, dead.

Danny turned expectantly to Geoff.

'Let, please.'

Jamie looked away. He knew Danny was not entitled to a let but he didn't expect a problem. Geoff was not a person to be fazed by anyone, not even Danny or his father.

'No let,' said Geoff.

▷ **5** *drive sth. – drove – driven:* make sth. move fast **8** *scuttle:* run quickly with short steps **10** *scoop sth. up:* lift sth. with a quick movement **12** *dive forward:* move quickly forward **15** *bellow* (v): make a loud sound **19** *curb sth.:* stop sth. **25** *poor:* bad **30** *impassive:* showing no feeling **30–31** *hewn marble:* aus Marmor gehauen **37** *leap – leapt – leapt:* jump **45** *jaded:* (here) tired because one has had enough of sth. **49** *tension:* Spannung · *temper sth.:* make sth. less unpleasant · *jubilation:* happiness, triumph **50** *ambition:* desire to be better or the best **55** *follow suit* [su:t]: do the same **58** *keep it tight:* (here) give your opponent little chance to hit a good shot · *plug sth.:* (here) hit sth. (esp. a ball) **62** *lunge* (v): move forward suddenly · *barge against sb.:* push against sb. **67** *be fazed by sb.:* be confused by sb.

'Oh, come on,' said Danny. 'He was just standing there. How am I supposed to get to the ball if he won't move out of the way?'

Jamie turned quietly to the side wall. He had heard this sort of dialogue so many times from Danny and, if it went on long enough, which it usually did, Bob Powell was bound to chime in.

'You were out of position,' said Geoff. 'You couldn't have reached the ball. I'm sorry. No let.'

Jamie picked up the ball with his racket and moved to the right-hand service box, ready to start. The accusation was unfounded but there was no point in saying anything. Danny was still glaring at Geoff.

'Tell me how I'm supposed to reach the ball with him plonked in the way.'

'I've given my decision. Play on, please.'

Sure enough, Bob Powell broke in.

'Pathetic. I've never seen such marking in all my life. The kid was blocking the way. Anyone could see it.'

Jamie said nothing and continued to wait, ball in hand. In a strange way, he was grateful for this interruption. It gave him a moment to catch his breath. But not for long. Geoff leaned on the rail and fixed his eyes on Danny.

'Danny, play on, please, or I'll award a penalty point.'

There were murmurs round the gallery as Danny, with a final glare, sloped into position to continue the match. Jamie served at once, hoping the incident would have unsettled Danny's rhythm.

But Danny was now fired up. The ball came back like a bullet. Jamie raced to the back and returned it down the side wall. Danny was onto it at once and cut it short across court.

Jamie lunged and sent the ball down the side wall. Danny cut it off and drove it across court. Jamie raced after it, caught it before it died and sent a back-wall boast flying over their heads to the front wall. Danny took it early, before it touched the floor, and sent it cutely into the forehand nick.

'That's the boy!' roared Powell.

Jamie glanced up and saw him flushed and jubilant, as though vindicated after a great injustice. But there was no time to think of that. Danny was already in the service box, chafing to finish the match. Jamie felt the spectre of defeat over him.

The serve came, a hard one this time, and aimed straight at him. He jumped to the side, too sluggishly – and the ball clipped the edge of his shorts. There was a gasp from above, then more cheers from Powell. Jamie looked down, ashamed.

He couldn't believe he'd let Danny catch him out like that.

'Four – love!' called Geoff.

Danny served from the left-hand box, another hard one straight at him. This time he was ready. He jumped to the side and drove the ball back. He desperately needed a point now to restore his confidence. But first he had to regain the serve.

Danny, however, seemed bent on denying him everything. The shots came back more crisply than ever and the pace and power which were Danny's trademark had returned. To Jamie, the next four points seemed to fly past in a maze of drives, volleys, and smashes that forced him back, yanked him forward, played with him like a toy. He knew then that he could not beat Danny. Not today. Perhaps not ever. Danny was too strong.

'Eight – love!' called Geoff. 'Game and match ball!'

Match ball. It seemed only moments ago that Geoff had called love – all in the first game of the match. He sensed the tension up in the gallery.

The serve came from the right-hand box, the first lob serve Danny had sent him for several rallies. Jamie stretched out and feebly tried to play a volley, though he had now ceased to care about the destiny of the restless little ball and wanted only to be free of it.

His wish was soon granted.

The ball climbed over his racket, dipped into the back corner and achieved what for him was the ultimate shame.

An ace.

He looked up at the gallery, searching the top right corner. And this time saw an empty space.

▷ **5** *chime in:* get involved **9** *unfounded:* wrong, not based on facts **11** *plonked:* (here) standing still and in the way **15** *pathetic:* stupid **18** *grateful:* feeling or showing thanks **22** *murmur* (n): low sound of surprise or disagreement **23** *slope* (v): (here): bend forward **31** *cutely:* precisely **34** *flushed:* red-faced **35** *vindicate sb.:* prove sb. right **36** *chafe* [tʃeɪf]: feel impatient **37** *spectre:* ghost **39** *sluggish:* slow · *clip sth.:* hit sth. lightly **40** *gasp* (n): sudden intake of breath **48** *be bent on sth.:* fest entschlossen sein, etwas zu tun · *deny sb. sth.:* not give sb. sth. **49** *crisp* (here): quick and precise · *pace:* speed **51** *maze:* confusion **52** *yank sb.:* pull sb. forcefully **60** *feeble:* weak **61** *cease to do sth.:* stop doing sth.

1 Strafpunkt

Joe and Andy clapped him on the back, told him he'd done well, that it was a terrific match. He didn't listen. He knew where he was meant to be and hurried on. Best to get it over with straight away. He hoped there would be no one in the changing room. Somehow it was always worse when they had to go to the back of the car park.

The changing room was empty. He walked to the centre of the room and waited, then the door opened behind him.

He stiffened and turned.

The hand flew out and struck him in the side of the face. His head flicked back, despite his efforts to keep it still. He cursed himself silently. He had told himself on the way here that this time he must not flinch. He forced his head forward, ready for the next one.

It came, the same cheek, but harder. There were no words, not yet. Later there would be words. There were always words, plenty of words. But not now.

His muscles tightened. There would be one more.

One for every game he'd lost today. The usual deal. And the last was always the hardest.

The hand lashed out; and this time he yelped. He looked down, breathing hard, then made himself straighten up.

But his father had already left the room.

1 anspannen

2 zurückzucken

Vater schlägt sohn für jedes verlorenes spiel

TWO

Ashingford seemed quiet for a Saturday evening and the December chill made it seem an even more lonely place. He trudged through the town centre, shifting the weight of his squash bag from one hand to the other and wishing he'd had the foresight to bring his coat. He should have known from bitter experience that Dad would make him walk home if he lost, with his kit, of course.

The punishments were predictable enough after all these years, as were the rewards. It was all a question of pass or fail, and the degree of effort involved, in Dad's eyes. A pass – in other words a win – meant money. Not as much as Danny would be getting from Bob Powell tonight in the usual ostentatious hand-out in the bar, but money nevertheless, and sometimes even words of praise, though, in keeping with Dad's relentlessly unforgiving standards, these were always tempered with exhortations to train harder, aim higher.

But a fail – that was different. A fail where Dad felt there was some effort involved meant extra workouts. A fail where he thought there was no effort meant …

He rubbed the side of his face and walked on, pushing the thoughts from his mind. The sprawling town centre fell away at last

▷ **12** *flinch:* move back from sth. unpleasant **19** *yelp* (v): cry out **23** *chill:* cold · *trudge* (v): walk slowly because you are tired **27** *kit:* sports clothes, etc. **28** *predictable:* vorhersehbar **29** *reward:* thing you are given because you have done sth. well **32** ostentatious [ˌɒstenˈteɪʃəs]: noticeable in a way that is intended to impress **33** *praise* [preɪz]: act of saying to a person that he or she has done well **33–34** *in keeping with sth.:* as is expected from sth. **34** *relentless:* not stopping **35** *exhortation:* Ermahnung **37** *workout:* period of physical training **40** *sprawling:* large and stretched out

and the estates opened up on either side of him. He left the clock tower behind him, wandered past the lane that ran down to the school and on as far as the station, then cut down the alleyway that tracked the railway line and came out at the bottom of their garden. He liked this way home, detached from the streets. It left him alone to think and he liked to come up to the back of his house through the allotments.

Suddenly he stopped.

Two men blocked his path a few feet away, one tall, the other slightly shorter and stockier. The darkness obscured their faces somewhat and he had little time to study them before they turned and moved to the side to let him pass. He did so, quickly, and hurried on, sensing their attention still upon him.

He didn't know why he felt uneasy. They hadn't challenged him but there was something about them he didn't trust. He knew this way home was not one his mother approved of. She worried about the more rowdy elements in the town and thought he shouldn't walk in places where he could be exposed to danger. But he had never felt danger here before.

He strode on a few more feet, then glanced over his shoulder.

They had not followed. But he had been right. Even in the darkness he sensed them watching.

He hurried on and didn't slow down until he saw the sheds dotted about the allotments on his left, and, to his right, the back gardens of the houses in his street. The wall of the alleyway came to an end and he started to relax a little. He liked this spot. Very few people came here and, with the allotments on one side and the gardens on the other, he could almost pretend he was in the country, though it took a good deal of pretending.

He reached their own patch of ground and gazed with some affection at the little shed at the bottom. It had become a kind of refuge. Dad wasn't keen on gardening and the allotment had always been Mum's special passion, but for some reason she seemed to have lost interest in it over the last year and since the shed was now rarely used, except to store sticks and plant pots and other gardening junk, he'd found it an excellent place to escape to when he wanted privacy. They never seemed to think of looking for him there. He'd had a duplicate key cut, secretly, and had left an old blanket and a tatty cushion there, hidden inside a bin bag and stuffed under some plant pots.

It was tempting to walk down there now, even in this cold weather. But that would only make things worse later.

He wandered up to the back gate of the house and stopped. Upstairs he could see a light on in Dad's study, and downstairs, Mum busy in the kitchen. He took a deep breath, tramped up to the house and opened the back door.

Mum looked round as he entered the kitchen.

'Darling, where have you been? I was expecting you ages ago.'

He frowned. 'I had to walk home.'

She looked at him for a moment, as though she wanted to say something, then leaned forward and gave him a hurried kiss.

'Well, never mind, you're here now and ...' She put on her oven gloves and opened the oven door. 'The food will probably ...'

She was doing it again: starting sentences and not finishing them. She'd only begun doing that recently. He stared at her, wondering whether Dad had hit her, too, tonight.

'Sit down, darling,' she said. She was smiling, but it was a distracted smile, a smile that barely had the energy to reach him. He sat down at the table, feeling numb and confused. An overdone lasagne appeared before him, followed by overdone carrots and overdone potatoes. He ate in silence.

Mum didn't ask about the squash.

Dad remained upstairs.

After supper he took the basketball, wandered out to the garden and threw the ball up at the basket on the wall. He often found it relaxing to come out here and throw a basketball and there was always the chance that the sound would bring Spider out from next door and they could talk.

▷ **1** *estate:* area consisting of lots of identical houses **3** *alleyway:* small narrow lane **4** *track sth.:* (here) go along beside sth. **5** *detached:* away **7** *allotment:* small piece of land for growing vegetables, etc. **10** *stocky:* short, with a strong, solid body **14** *uneasy:* worried or unhappy **16** *approve of sth.:* think sth. is good **23–24** *dotted about sth.:* situated in or around sth. **30** *gaze* (v): give a long steady look **31** *refuge* ['refju:dʒ] place to go to for protection **38** *tatty* (infml): shabby **39** *bin bag:* plastic bag for rubbish **47** *ages ago* (infml): a long time ago **48** *frown* [fraʊn]: die Stirn runzeln **57** *distracted:* not paying attention because one is worried **58** *numb* [nʌm]: without feeling · *overdone:* cooked too long

But there was no light at his friend's window. Suddenly he heard footsteps at the bottom of the garden. He whirled round, thinking of Spider.

But it was not Spider.

It was a figure moving past the gate. The face turned for an instant and Jamie drew breath. It was one of the men he had seen earlier, the taller one. There was no mistaking him, even in the darkness. Their eyes met, briefly, then the man passed from view.

Jamie stood there, still holding the basketball and wondering why he felt so nervous. There was no reason why this person shouldn't be walking round here at nine o'clock at night. But he wondered where the other man was.

Then he saw him.

Down among the sheds at the foot of the allotments was the shorter, stockier figure, also unmistakable. A few moments later the tall man joined him and the two stood there for several minutes, seemingly in conversation, though Jamie caught no words.

Then, with a glance in his direction, they turned and were gone.

THREE

'I've come to a decision,' said Dad over breakfast. 'I'm stopping your money.'

Jamie stared at him, then at Mum. But she was avoiding both their eyes. He sensed that she and Dad had already argued over this; and he would have come off best as usual.

'You're not winning,' Dad went on. 'I don't know why. You should be. Your last six opponents – apart from Danny – were all worse players than you. And you should have taken Danny apart in that third game, like you did in the first and second. I don't know what's got into you.'

Jamie looked away. He hated the money side of squash. But Dad wasn't talking about the win bonuses, as he liked to call them.

'I'm talking about your pocket money. It's time you started winning again so the win bonuses stay. But no pocket money. You're on commission only.'

'That's not fair. You know it's not.'

'It's perfectly fair and that's the way it'll be. When you start playing the way you should, I'll reinstate the pocket money.'

'So I'm to get nothing at all. Unless I go out and get a job.'

'You've already got a job – to improve your squash and start playing to your potential.'

'And what do I do if I want to go and see a film with Spider?'

▷ **2** *whirl:* turn round quickly **8** *brief:* short, quick **26** *take sb. apart* (infml): defeat sb. easily **33** *be on commission:* (here) receive money only when one shows results **36** *reinstate sth.* [ˌriːɪnˈsteɪt]: start sth. up again

'You shouldn't be wasting your time with that boy anyway. He's a loser. He's going nowhere.'

'Well, somebody else, then?'

Dad merely shrugged. 'You'll just have to start winning matches again.'

Jamie felt anger rise within him. He had to have money. The win bonuses were useful but even after a string of losses, he had always had the lifeline of pocket money.

Dad stood up from the table.

'I know you think this is hard. But you're not going to get where you want to go without making some sacrifices. You'll thank me for this one day.' He looked at his watch. 'You'd better get ready. We're behind already this morning.'

Half an hour later, he and Dad were driving in through the school gates.

Years ago, in the days when he'd enjoyed squash, he had thought it a good thing that his school had its own squash court, grotty though it was. And Dad being Chairman of Governors as well as a former squash celebrity and a highly successful writer of motivational books, not to mention a close personal friend of Mr Talbot, the headmaster, himself a squash fanatic, meant that they had their own key and could use the court whenever they liked.

Especially since Dad had said publicly on numerous occasions that his son would one day turn professional and become world champion. Big words, and they always made Jamie cringe when he heard them, but Dad believed in talking that way. For him, everything came down to visualizing the goal, affirming that it's going to happen, then working hard to achieve it.

World Champion. It seemed a crazy ambition but Dad kept telling him he could make it. And sometimes, when he played, and the game went well, he almost felt he could do it. He knew he was good. But what frightened him was how much each match now cost him.

They pulled up outside the squash court. Dad switched off the engine and swivelled round in the seat. Jamie looked at him and knew what was coming. Sure enough, it was smile-time.

'You think I'm being hard on you, don't you?' said Dad.

Jamie said nothing. Dad put an arm round him.

'You've got to understand, I don't hit you because I like it. I hit you because it'll help you. One of these days you'll be a father and you'll know what I'm talking about. There'll be times when you can see your boy's going wrong and the only way to correct it is with a short, sharp shock.'

And Mum? he thought. Does she need a short, sharp shock every time you hit her? But he said nothing, knowing what the response would be. Dad squeezed him.

'I know it's hard for you to understand what I'm aiming at. But you've just got to trust my judgement. When I was your age, I had no one to help me. I had to find my own way. There were lots of times when I ... are you listening to this?'

Jamie started at the sudden change of tone. Having heard these words so many times, his mind had drifted to thoughts of the two men and, more importantly, his worries about money. He quickly managed a half-smile.

'Sorry.'

Dad looked hard at him for a moment and Jamie wondered what was in his mind. He wished he could be close to his father, like Spider was with his. Dad squeezed him again.

'Let's get started.'

They climbed out of the car and Jamie went round to the boot to fetch the gear while Dad unlocked the court. The little building looked drab, especially on this miserable December morning, and there was an air of depression about the place. But at least it was never cold. The heating system that fed the court was so antiquated that it could not be properly regulated. When it was on, it was uncomfortably hot but since he never played matches here, it didn't matter too much. And in cold weather like this he was grateful for the warmth.

He picked up his racket and fiddled with the strings, unwilling to get started.

▷ **4** *shrug* (v): mit den Achseln zucken **8** *lifeline:* thing which you depend on **11** *make sacrifices:* give up important things in order to achieve certain aims **17** *grotty* (infml): unpleasant, in a bad state **18** *(Board of) Governors*: group of people who determine how a school is run **19** *motivational book:* book that inspires readers to achieve sth. **25** *cringe:* feel very embarrassed and uncomfortable **27** *come down to sth:* be able to be explained by sth. simply · *visualize sth.:* imagine sth. **34** *swivel* ['swɪvl] (v): turn around **45** *squeeze sb./sth.:* press sb./sth. with your arms (here) to indicate a feeling of closeness **50** *start at sth.:* make a sudden movement out of surprise or fear because of sth. **59** *boot* (BE): Kofferraum **60** *gear:* sports equipment and clothes, etc. **61** *drab:* colourless **67** *fiddle with sth.:* play around with sth.

'Never mind the racket,' said Dad. 'Get on with your stretching exercises while I warm the ball up.'

He went through the stretching routine, glancing now and then at his father driving the ball rhythmically against the front wall. Even now Dad looked immaculate on court, though well past his prime and with his body broken by the over-training of his youth, not to mention the knee injury that prematurely cut short his brilliant playing career. All his shots were grooved, precise, economical. There were no frills. His body position was always perfect, though he moved sluggishly now.

Like greased lightning, he used to be, Mum always said, and Jamie wondered how he would have fared in a match with his father, had Dad been sixteen now. He finished his exercises and stepped forward, unable to put things off any longer. Dad said nothing and merely hit the ball to him, and for a few minutes they warmed up together, neither speaking as they drove the ball across court to each other.

'Change,' muttered Dad after a few minutes, and he moved across and they repeated the procedure on the other side. This was usually the silent time. They would warm up slowly, then it would be boasts and drives followed by the rest of the practice routines and finally ghosting – simulated squash without the ball – which he hated.

Dad grunted, the signal to start the boasts and drives, and Jamie went forward. Having spent so much time on court together, they hardly needed to speak now and Dad didn't usually bother to announce the next thing. They both knew the sequence so well.

He started the routine, driving the ball down the forehand side wall, moving back to the T position, forward to the backhand wall to pick up the shot his father had boasted to him from the back of the court, then driving it hard down that side, and so on, ad nauseam; though, in reality, he quite liked this routine. The only thing that stopped it being properly enjoyable was the thought of all the more torturous routines to come.

Yet even as he ran and hit and sweated and lunged, he found his thoughts wandering again. To the problem of money.

And the two strange men.

Spider opened the front door and looked him over in his quizzical way.

'And what do you want, disturbing me on a Sunday afternoon?'

Jamie managed a smile. 'Fancy a walk into town?'

'To see the tourist attractions?'

'What tourist attractions?'

'Well, give me a couple of hours and I'll come up with something. Suppose your dad's out or he'd never approve of this.'

Jamie felt himself flush. It always made him uncomfortable when Spider commented on Dad's disapproval, not that his friend was the slightest bit bothered whether anyone approved of him or not. That was one of the refreshing things about him.

Spider shrugged.

'I suppose I can put up with you for a couple of hours, as long as you don't get too paranoid and moody. Got any money?'

Jamie looked down. 'No.'

'What a surprise. Well, come in, anyway. It's freezing.'

He entered the house and Spider closed the door behind him.

'So did you win?'

Jamie shook his head.

'Oh, dear,' said Spider. 'I've got to be nice to you. What was the score?'

'What do you care? You hate squash.'

'I don't hate squash. I'm just bored by it. There's a difference. Boredom doesn't require effort. Hatred does. Can't stand effort.'

'I had noticed.'

'Good God, humour. There's hope for you yet. What was the score?'

'Three-two to him.'

'And who's him?'

'Boy called Danny. You wouldn't know him. He doesn't go to our school.'

'Is that the one who acts the prima donna on court?'

'There are lots of people who do that.'

▷ **5** *immaculate:* perfect · *prime:* physically the best years of one's life **7** *premature:* happening before the expected time **8** *grooved:* (here) well-placed or hit well **9** *frills:* (here) things that look attractive but are unnecessary **11** *greased lightning:* geölter Blitz **12** *fare:* get on **14** *put sth. off:* delay doing sth. **29** *ad nauseam* (Latin): up to the point of being totally boring **32** *torturous* ['tɔːtʃərəs]: extremely unpleasant **49** *put up with sb./sth.:* tolerate sb./sth. **50** *moody:* showing that one is feeling depressed

'But he's the one who beat you three–nil last time, right?'

'Three–love.'

'Three–love. You told me about it. He messed about during the match and accused you of gamesmanship or something.'

Jamie nodded. 'That was him.'

'Have you ever beaten him?'

'No. I've come close lots of times. People keep telling me if I could just be more aggressive on court, I'd take him apart.'

'And would you?'

'Maybe.' Jamie paused. 'I just ... can't work up aggression that easily. And if you're too aggresive, your strokes and tactics can go to pieces. I usually manage to get fired up for a couple of games and, when I do, things go pretty well. But I can't keep it going. I seem to bottle out when it really counts.'

'Oh, well. Beat him next time. When are you playing him again?'

'Two weeks. The Regional Championships. Of all the coincidences.'

'What do you mean?'

'Well, since we've both had our birthdays, we no longer qualify as under sixteens. We've had to join the under nineteens.'

'What's wrong with that?'

'Nothing. It's just that when we were under sixteens, he was seeded one in the county and I was seeded two.'

'I thought you were number one.'

'I was number one until Danny moved down here.'

Jamie paused again, thinking of the things Dad had said to him on the day he lost the number one spot; and the things he had said since. 'Anyway,' he went on, 'because of the way we were seeded, we usually met in the final at the Regional Championships. But now that we've joined the under nineteens, where the standard's much higher and you're up against the likes of Andy Bailey –'

'Who's he?'

'Boy at the squash club. Eighteen. Brilliant player.'

'Another prima donna?'

'No, he's OK. I like him. But because there are more players like Andy around, Danny and I are now seeded lower and it was about a one in God-knows-how-many chance for us to be drawn to meet in the first round of this year's regionals. And guess what's happened?'

Spider reached for his coat.

'Well, you'll just have to beat him, then, won't you? Are these Regional Championships important?'

'Fairly. And they're a sort of warm up for January.'

'January?'

'The Junior Open. The World Championships.'

Spider looked at him in silence for a moment.

'All these tournaments you go to. You're always off somewhere.'

Jamie frowned. Spider was right. There were so many tournaments about the country and Dad dragged him round most of them. It was supposed to improve his ranking, his match play, his temperament, but he knew that in reality it did none of those things. For him, at least. All that happened was that he played and lost.

They walked through to the front room where he heard sounds of laughter.

'What's going on?' he said.

'The twins were ten yesterday. We've been eating the leftovers of the party.'

Jamie entered the front room and saw Mr and Mrs Dean on the floor with Amy and Becky, plates and bottles and plastic cups all around them. He loved coming here. It was so unlike the atmosphere in his own house where everything was obsessively neat and life was geared only to squash. The Deans, by contrast, seemed to live in a state of permanent chaos and took people and events as they came, no questions asked and no judgements made.

'Jamie!' shouted Mr Dean. 'How are you?'

'He's not very happy,' said Spider.

'Why not?'

'He lost.'

'Lost what?'

Spider looked at Jamie and laughed.

'Sorry, but squash isn't top priority in this household.'

▷ **1** *nil:* (in football and other games except squash and tennis) a score of zero points **3** *mess about:* (here) behave badly **4** *gamesmanship:* type of unfair play that involves making the opponent unsure of him- or herself **14** *bottle out* (infml): lose courage **16** *of all the …:* so ein … **16–17** *coincidence* [kəʊˈɪnsɪdəns]: accidental, unexpected happening **22** *seed sb.:* (im Tennis und Squash) jdn. setzen, platzieren **31** *the likes of sb.:* people as good as sb. **37** *be drawn:* (here) be chosen in a lottery system **49** *ranking:* person's position on a scale that shows how good they are compared to others · *temperament:* control of emotions **61** *be geared to sth.:* be centred around sth.

'Squash?' Mr Dean looked across. 'You lost at squash?'

'Yes,' said Jamie.

Mrs Dean stood up.

'Never mind, Jamie. Would you like some cake?'

'He hasn't got time for cake,' said Spider. 'We're walking into Ashingford.'

Mrs Dean cuffed Spider, then looked back at Jamie.

'We'll just rewind and try that again. Jamie, would you like some cake?'

'No, thanks.'

'Don't take any notice of Spider. He's above himself because he's gone and got another job.' She frowned. 'Yet another. Don't ask me how he's going to fit his homework in round all the things he's doing.'

Jamie looked at Spider.

'So what's this one?'

'It's only part-time. Saturdays and after school some days.'

'But what is it?'

'Stock replenishment executive.'

'What?'

'Stock replenishment executive.'

Jamie stared at him. 'Is that what I think it is?'

Mrs Dean pushed Spider to the side and took Jamie by the arm.

'He's a shelf-stacker at the supermarket. As if he hasn't earned enough money already towards this wretched car.'

'That's just the point,' said Spider. 'I haven't earned enough. I want to save up more to put towards lessons when I'm seventeen, and any repair bills and stuff like that.'

Mr Dean snorted.

'Why's it got to be a sports car? What's wrong with an old banger? That was always good enough for me.'

'It shows,' said Spider.

Jamie chuckled, having heard variations of this discussion so many times. Spider had been single-mindedly saving since he was twelve towards the dream car he intended to buy in time for his seventeenth birthday and had had a succession of jobs over the years, often two or three at the same time. He made no secret to Jamie or anyone else of how much he had saved, and it was now a considerable amount of money. It often amused – and sometimes irritated – Jamie that his friend's dry and laid-back manner caused so many people – especially Dad – to misjudge him and think he had no motivation.

Not that Spider cared.

'He's obsessed with money,' said Mr Dean. 'I think he's trying to become a magnate.'

'What's a magnate?' said Amy, her mouth full of cake.

Becky looked round at her. 'You pick up metal with it.'

Mrs Dean laughed.

'He's transferred all his money from the building society into his bank account so that he's got it ready the moment he wants to make an offer, and he's actually started going out looking at some of the cars he's interested in, which means his dad has to go with him, or I do, so that someone can drive the car. Then he's not happy because he doesn't think we're giving the car a proper test run.'

'What's a proper test run?' said Jamie.

'A fast test run,' said Mr Dean. 'I can't work out how a boy who takes three hours to get dressed in the mornings wants a car that screams out of the blocks like a bat out of hell. Thank God he hasn't found the one he wants yet.'

Mrs Dean chuckled.

'Anyway, Jamie – tea?'

He glanced at Spider.

'No, thanks. We were ...going into town.'

'There won't be much open this afternoon.'

'The fast food's open,' said Spider. 'We can get a milk shake or something.'

Mr Dean pointed a chocolate finger biscuit at Jamie.

'Well, make sure Spider pays for something. Becky, don't do that with the jelly.'

Spider took him by the arm. 'Come on, let's get out of here.'

▷ **7** *cuff sb.:* give sb. a light blow with the hand **18** *stock:* the goods that a shop has on its shelves · *replenish sth.* [rɪ'plenɪʃ]: refill sth. (e.g. a shelf that has become empty) · *executive* [ɪg'zekjətɪv]: manager **23** *shelf-stacker:* person who puts goods on shelves in a shop · *earn sth.:* get sth. by working **24** *wretched* ['retʃid]: terrible **26** *lesson:* (here) driving lesson **29** *banger* (infml): old car that makes a lot of noise **31** *it shows:* you can see that **33** *single-minded:* thinking only of one thing **39** *laid-back* (infml): relaxed **44** *magnate* ['mægneɪt]: a rich and powerful businessman (Becky confuses the word with 'magnet') **53** *proper:* correct **57** *scream out of the blocks:* starts so quickly it makes a loud noise · *bat:* Fledermaus **66** *finger biscuit:* biscuit shaped like a finger

FOUR

They walked down the road, burying their chins in their scarves. The cold snap that had set in since the beginning of December seemed set to continue and, if anything, was growing worse.

'Not sure this is a good idea,' said Spider. 'Think I'll go for a hot chocolate instead of a milk shake. If we make it there without turning back.'

They made their way towards the town centre.

'So, this Danny,' said Spider. 'Where does he go to school?'

'Fairways.'

'Oh, *Fair-ways*!' Spider twitched up his nose. 'No wonder we haven't seen him at our school. His folks must be well off.'

'His dad's loaded.'

'He'd have to be. So what's he like? Apart from being a pain on court.'

'I don't know him that well. I just see him up at the club or on the playing circuit. I don't know where he lives or what kind of family he's got. They came down from up north a year ago. I know his dad. He comes to watch everything.'

'And what's he like?'

'Obnoxious. He and my dad hate each other.'

'I wonder why,' said Spider, his face deadpan. 'Still, just as well you don't know the rest of the family. They're probably obnoxious, too.'

'If there are any others. I told you, I don't know anything about them. Don't particularly want to.'

They passed the clock tower and turned down the main street, walking faster as they grew colder. The traffic was heavier here, even on a Sunday, and there were cars parked on both sides of the road. Spider broke into a trot.

'Come on, I can't stand any more of this.'

And they ran the last few hundred yards.

Rossi's Burger Bonanza was not the most up-market of establishments but on a day as cold as this, they were grateful for it. Spider hurried up to the counter, took off his gloves and looked round at him.

'So you haven't got any money?'

'Sorry.'

'What do you want, then?'

'Just a hot chocolate. Thanks.'

'Don't you want any chips?'

'No, thanks.'

'I'm having some.'

'You've just been eating cake and jelly.'

'What's that got to do with it?' He looked at the assistant. 'Two hot chocolates and two large chips, please. To eat here.'

Jamie looked at him. 'But I said –'

Spider stopped him with a glance. 'Your stomach said something else. Do something useful and look for a table.'

Jamie found one upstairs overlooking the street and stood by it for a moment, thinking. He hated being bailed out by Spider, who, despite Mr Dean's jokes, was always generous with his money. But he knew he couldn't go on like this. There had to be a way of getting money of his own – and not from playing squash. Suddenly he stiffened.

The two men had appeared in the street below. He recognized them at once, even though he had only seen them in the darkness before. He moved back from the window but kept his eyes upon them.

Spider appeared with a tray.

'There you go,' he said, holding out one of the cartons of chips.

▷ **1** *scarf:* Schal **2** *cold snap:* period of cold weather **12** *loaded* (infml): very rich **13** *pain* (infml): very unpleasant or annoying person **16** *playing circuit* ['sɜːkɪt]: the different clubs where contests take place **20** *obnoxious* [əb'nɒkʃəs]: very unpleasant **21** *deadpan:* showing no emotion **31** *up-market:* chic, trendy **49** *bail sb. out* (infml): pay sb.'s expenses

'Thanks.' Jamie took the chips absentmindedly, his eyes still on the street.

'What are you looking at?' said Spider.

Jamie snapped out of his reverie.

'Oh, nothing. Just ... looking.' He sat down quickly. 'So, what's this job like, then?'

'Pretty boring. Just a means to an end. But we have some fun, too. And there's some nice girls there. Not that you'd be interested, being married to squash.'

'Very funny.'

He looked away, feeling awkward again. He wished he could be like Spider. Spider always seemed so comfortable in his own skin. He was never fazed by anything and seemed to coast through life, unaffected by all the worries he himself felt burdened with. No wonder Spider had lots of friends while he had only one. And that was Spider.

He stiffened again.

The men had appeared downstairs and were standing at the counter, talking to one of the assistants. He could just see them through the gap where the stairway twisted round. They didn't seem to be ordering food.

'What's up?' said Spider.

Jamie glanced at him, then back at the two men.

'Nothing, I just ...' He made up his mind. 'I've just got to go to the loo.'

'OK.'

He jumped to his feet and made his way downstairs, trying not to look hurried. Crazy though it was, he knew he had to get close to these men, without making them aware of him. He didn't want them to recognize him from yesterday, yet he had to satisfy his curiosity and hear what they were saying.

He joined the back of the nearest queue and studied them surreptitiously. They certainly weren't short of money, judging from the stylish clothing, and the watches and rings they both sported. The taller one seemed about twenty-five and stood out more, not merely by virtue of his height but by a certain air and swarthy good looks. The shorter man seemed older, perhaps because he was balding; but Jamie disliked him more.

He knew this suspicion was probably unfounded, yet something about the men still disturbed him. He leaned forward, trying to catch some of their words while holding himself in readiness to turn his back if they looked round. But they were already at the end of their conversation.

'OK,' said the tall one to the assistant. 'Well, let us know if you do. The phone number's on the card.'

And, a moment later, they had walked past him and were gone.

He watched them for a while as they sauntered off down the street, then he hurried back upstairs. Spider's eyes were bright with amusement.

'You losing your marbles?'

'What?'

'You walked right past the loo.'

'Oh.' He tried to look unconcerned. 'Yeah, I forgot.'

'So aren't you going?'

'No, I can't be bothered. Let's just eat.'

Spider raised an eyebrow but said no more.

It was six o'clock when he arrived home and he knew at once that something was wrong. Dad was standing before him in the hall, scowling.

'Why did you take the money from your mother's purse?'

Jamie stared at him. Somewhere upstairs he heard Mum crying.

'I ... I didn't take any money.'

'So why is there money missing?'

'I don't know.'

Dad took a step forward.

'There were three notes in your mother's purse. They're all gone.'

▷ **4** *reverie* ['revəri]: state of thinking deeply about sth. **7** *a means to an end:* a thing that helps one to do sth. more important **13** *coast through sth.:* move easily through sth. **14** *unaffected:* untouched · *burden sb. with sth.:* give sb. sth. (esp. work or responsibility) that makes them worry **25** *loo* (infml): toilet **33** *surreptitious* [ˌsʌrəp'tɪʃəs]: done carefully or secretly **34** *sport sth.:* wear sth. **36** *by virtue of sth.:* because of sth. · *air:* feeling or impression given by sb. · *swarthy:* (of a person) dark in colour **37** *balding:* losing one's hair **39** *suspicion:* feeling that sb. has done sth. wrong **47** *saunter* ['sɔːntə]: walk without hurrying **50** *lose your marbles* (infml): become unable to think properly **53** *unconcerned:* not worried about sth. **55** *not be bothered:* not care enough **59** *scowl* [skaʊl]: show anger in one's face

Jamie moved back towards the door. He knew why suspicion fell on him but this was too much. His father's hand lashed out. Jamie ducked, just in time, and raced out into the street.

He knew this would do him no good but he couldn't stop himself. To be denied money was bad enough; to be unjustly accused of stealing it was worse. He ran to the end of the road and cut back towards the alleyway behind the houses. There was only one refuge he knew of, cold though it would be.

He reached the allotments, slowed down and padded between the sheds until he reached their own. It looked chilly and uninviting in the darkness but he knew of no other sanctuary right now. He lifted the stone under which he hid his duplicate key, then gave a start.

The padlock was lying on the ground close by and beside it a small iron bar. He straightened up and stared at the latch. It had been forced. Cautiously he opened the door and peeped in.

There was no one there. But in the corner where he liked to sit, he could see the old blanket and tatty cushion on the floor. And he distinctly remembered leaving them in the bin bag last time he was here.

But he couldn't think about that now. He closed the door behind him and stood there for a moment, enveloped in blackness, trying to calm his racing thoughts; then he wrapped the blanket round him, propped the cushion under his head, and lay back in the dark.

FIVE

In the night he heard voices. He lay as still as he could, though he was shivering uncontrollably now and desperately anxious to go back to the house. But there was a coldness there he feared even more than this.

The voices came closer, then, to his relief, faded away.

He thought of Mum crying and wondered what had happened. But it was easy enough to guess. Dad would have first accused her of losing the money. Then he would have hit her. And finally, having presumably decided she was telling the truth, he would have jumped to the next conclusion.

Mum would receive flowers in the morning, of course, and the usual note saying how wonderful she was. As for himself …

He bit his lip and pulled his coat more tightly around him. It was no use trying to think about the future when the present demanded all his attention. Suddenly he heard a new sound.

Footsteps.

He held himself rigid, wondering who it could be. A few seconds later, a hand fiddled with the latch.

He sat up, trying to keep quiet. The door opened a fraction and he sensed a dark form there. He thought of the blanket and cushion that

▷ **3** *duck* (v): avoid being hit by moving your head or upper body downward **9** *pad* (v): walk softly **11** *sanctuary:* place where one is safe **13** *padlock:* special kind of lock attached to a door **14** *latch:* Riegel **15** *cautious* ['kɔːʃəs]: careful **21** *enveloped in sth.* [ɪn'veləpt]: surrounded by sth. **32** *presumably:* probably **32–33** *jump to a conclusion:* come to an opinion about sth. too quickly, without really thinking

had been moved. If this were a tramp returning, there could be trouble. Tramps might be violent if they found a squat taken over. The door opened wider and moonlight fell upon the figure.

He gasped.

It was a girl.

He must have moved or made some sound, as she turned at once and rushed away. He jumped to his feet, startled, and plunged out into the chill of the night. She was stumbling off across the allotments, running awkwardly as though in pain.

'Wait!' He called out, as loudly as he dared, not wanting to draw attention from the house. She did not stop. He hurried after her and caught her up. 'Please wait. I don't mean you any harm.'

She stopped and turned round. 'What makes you think I'm scared of you?'

He stared at her, unsure what to say. 'Well, you're … I mean, you're running away.'

She looked him over scornfully. 'Don't flatter yourself I'm bothered about you.'

He frowned, unsure whether to turn and leave her. She obviously wanted nothing to do with him, and he had enough problems of his own. He studied her, warily.

She seemed about his age and he wondered what she was doing wandering about this place on a cold December night. She was wearing a short jacket, which didn't look as though it afforded her much warmth, a longish skirt and a thick pullover, and high boots. Her hair was straight and ran down as far as her shoulders and she had a woollen hat on that made her look somewhat mischievous. Her face, with its small mouth, impish nose and bright eyes, would normally have been attractive to him, in a wild kind of way, had there not been so much defiance in it. She was carrying a battered-looking holdall.

She turned to walk on and he caught her profile. He drew breath. She was pregnant.

Heavily pregnant, too, by the look of it. He knew little enough about such things but even he could tell that this girl could not have long to wait before she gave birth.

He spoke again.

'Listen, I'm sorry I startled you. If you've been using the shed, that's OK. I was just … I mean … if you want to have it back for a while –'

'What were you doing there?' she said.

He looked away. He wasn't sure he wanted to give any explanations to a strange girl. But he didn't have to tell her he lived close by.

'I've fallen out with my dad,' he said.

She said nothing but started to walk back towards the shed. He followed her, still wondering whether to leave or stay. But he didn't know where else he could go now. All he knew was that he couldn't go back home, not as things stood. He glanced at the house and saw a light on in his room. They were still up, though there was no one at the window. He glanced at his watch and saw it was two o'clock.

Two in the morning and here he was, tired, hungry, cold, following some vagrant girl towards an allotment shed. She didn't slow down for him to catch her up but she wasn't looking over her shoulder so he assumed she trusted him a little. She reached the shed first and walked straight in without a backward glance.

Maybe this was how things were for those sleeping rough. You took what you could while it was there. If someone else took your doss, you fought them for it or found another place. Or came back later and reclaimed it.

He entered the shed and looked towards the corner. She didn't seem afraid of him; indeed, she appeared hardly to notice him now. She had pulled an old blanket from her bag and, together with his own blanket and the cushion, was awkwardly trying to make herself comfortable. She didn't look towards him as he stood in the doorway.

Then, to his surprise, she spoke. 'Thanks for giving up your place.'

It wasn't a soft voice – but it wasn't a hard voice, either. It was a tired voice, a voice that spoke of pain. He thought for a moment, then, remembering the other voices he had heard, answered her.

▷ **2** *squat* (n): place where a person lives illegally **4** *gasp* (v): take a quick deep breath because of surprise or fear **7** *startled:* surprised and frightened **17** *scornful:* without respect · *flatter sb.:* think too well of sb. **21** *wary* ['weəri]: cautious, careful when dealing with sb. **24** *afford sb. sth.:* give sb. sth. **27** *mischievous* ['mɪstʃɪvəs]: enjoying causing trouble **28** *impish:* showing an amusing lack of respect **30** *defiance* [dɪ'faɪəns]: resistance · *battered:* old, used a lot and shabby **31** *holdall:* type of large bag **33** *pregnant:* expecting a baby **44** *fall out with sb.:* have a serious quarrel with sb. **52** *vagrant* ['veɪgrənt] (adj): homeless **54** *assume sth.:* suppose sth. **56** *sleep rough* (infml): sleep outdoors in any place that you find because you have no home **58** *doss* (infml): sleeping-place **59** *reclaim sth.:* take sth. back that had been taken away

'Listen, I'm going to close the door to keep out the chill, all right? That's all I'm doing it for.'

She said nothing and he took that as consent.

He closed the door and blackness fell once more on the inside of the shed. He sat down on the wooden floor, close to the door. It was cold and there was a steady draught that ran over his back. He shifted to try and avoid it, but without success. She spoke again.

'You can move round this side if you want.'

He looked over towards her. There was precious little room for two people where she was but he needed no further persuasion to get away from the draught. He crawled slowly towards her, trying not to startle her by making any sudden movements. She reached out and pushed some of the plant pots to the side to clear a space. He sat down on the floor, his back against the same wall as her, and stretched his legs out alongside hers.

He still felt cold but it was a little better. She didn't speak and neither did he. He desperately needed to think. He couldn't stay here indefinitely. Sooner or later he would have to go and face his father and sort out the business with the money, and make sure Mum was OK.

Yet, strangely, he also felt he had to do something to help this girl.

He knew it was stupid even to think of getting involved. She probably couldn't wait to see the back of him. He found himself wondering about the baby and stole a glance at her. She was staring up at the roof of the shed, seemingly lost in thought. He hesitated.

'Shouldn't you … I mean … shouldn't you be in hospital or something?'

'Shouldn't you be minding your own business or something?'

The response came back as sharp as a knife. And he understood well enough. No questions, then. And that was fair enough. He didn't want to talk about himself, either. At least, not much. But one question was surely OK.

'Can I ask your name?'

'You can ask.'

He looked away.

No names either, then. He thought for a moment, wondering whether to give his own name, anyway. But he said nothing and she remained silent, too. He was shivering more and more now and wondering whether he would be able to stick the night out like this.

The thought of going back to the house sickened him. It would be like defeat. But if he didn't stop shivering soon, he would have to consider it, whatever the consequences.

She spoke suddenly. 'You'd better share this a bit.'

She was spreading the blankets his way. He tried to wrap himself up in them but still felt freezing and imagined she did, too, though she said nothing and simply lay on her back, staring as before up at the roof of the shed. Even so, he sensed she was keeping a furtive eye on him.

He tried to settle himself to sleep, but it was no good. The chill seemed to cut through body and mind. Suddenly he realized she had turned to face him.

'Listen,' she said abruptly, 'we'll get through this better if we lean our bodies together.'

'OK.'

'But I'm telling you, if you start –'

'It's OK. You don't need to worry.'

'I might be pregnant but I can take care of myself.'

'I told you – it's OK. We don't have to lie together at all if you don't want to.'

He wasn't sure he wanted to now, though he knew she was right. It was probably the only way they would get through tonight. She eyed him a moment longer, then moved slowly towards him.

'Just remember what I said,' she muttered.

He didn't answer but moved cautiously closer, keeping his arms at his sides. Their bodies touched, arm to arm first, then, after some hesitant shuffling, hip to hip, leg to leg. He held himself rigidly still, aware of her softness, even as he felt the tension in her and realized, with relief, that, for all her talk, she was as wary of him as he was of her.

He didn't know whether she was dangerous. Perhaps she was. She might have a knife hidden somewhere but, whatever the case, he didn't imagine she would be looking for trouble in her present state. Whatever she said, she must surely feel vulnerable.

▷ **3** *consent:* agreement **6** *draught* [drɑ:ft]: flow of air **9** *precious little* (infml): hardly enough **10** *persuasion:* act of giving reasons for sb. to do sth. **18** *indefinitely:* for an unlimited time **22** *get involved:* take an active personal interest (in sth.) **39** *stick the night out* (infml): stay the night in a place that is uncomfortable, etc. **47** *sense sth.:* feel sth. · *furtive:* secret **66** *shuffle:* move things against each other **72** *vulnerable:* easily hurt

They lay rigidly still for some minutes, neither talking, neither moving. Her body did indeed take away some of the chill, as did the blankets, but he was still horribly cold. After a while, he felt her stir.

'Put your arm round me,' she said. 'And remember, don't –'

'Yeah, yeah.'

He pulled his arm up from his side, reached carefully over her shoulder and let it rest down the other side of her body, but without touching her. She seemed reassured by this and moved her head into the crook of his arm, then, after a few more minutes, onto his chest. He felt her hair brush against his nose and moved his head back to stop it tickling. She moved no more and neither did he. For some reason he found himself strangely aware of the bulge in her belly, though he could not see it and did not touch it.

She was right. They were warmer together. Parts of him were still very cold but he did not dare bring his body fully round against hers, though he wanted to. She, clearly, had no such intention, either. They lay there, in silence, and somehow, against all the odds, he fell asleep.

SIX

When he awoke, the girl was gone. And he saw daylight under the door.

He was still cold, hungry, upset. He stretched and felt a crick in his neck, then sat up and tried to think. He was not ready to face Dad. while part of him yearned to stride into the house and find out if Mum was all right, not to mention attack the contents of the fridge, a greater part still boiled with anger and hurt.

He pressed the light-button on his watch. Ten to nine. It didn't seem possible that he'd managed to sleep through the cold. He thought of Spider. His friend wouldn't have waited for him this morning and he certainly wouldn't have called at the house, knowing he was unpopular with Dad.

Jamie yawned. There was only one place to go, though it was no solution and would only postpone the moment of reckoning a little bit. But at least he would be warm there.

He stood up, walked over to the door and peeped out, then, seeing no one, slipped out and hurried away across the allotment.

He arrived at school at half-past nine and made his way straight to room eleven. He knew he should have reported to the office but he

▷ **3** *stir:* move **9** *the crook of one's arm:* the inside of the circle made by an arm bent at the elbow **12** *bulge* (n): thing that sticks out **17** *against all the odds:* in spite of all the difficulties **22** *crick:* sudden and painful stiff feeling in the muscles of your neck **22** *yearn to do sth.:* want to do sth. very much **24** *boil with anger:* be very angry **36** *postpone sth.:* arrange for sth. to happen later **41** *report to the office:* sich im Schulbüro melden

no longer cared about rules. He needed to sit down, he needed to be somewhere warm, he needed to see Spider. He wanted his friend by him, at least for a few minutes, before Dad caught up with him.

He stopped outside room eleven and listened to Mrs Campbell's voice. He hated German, not just because he was no good at it but because Mrs Campbell seemed to whine at him all the time. But then, lots of the teachers had started whining at him over the past year. And it was only recently that he had noticed that their whining coincided with the increase in training Dad had been demanding of him. But there was no point in dwelling on that now.

He took a deep breath and opened the door.

Faces turned towards him as he entered the room. Mrs Campbell looked him over.

'You're very late, Jamie. I presume you have a reason?'

'Yes, miss.' He couldn't be bothered to invent one. All he wanted to do was sit down and be left to himself. He saw Spider watching him from the corner. Mrs Campbell spoke again.

'And what is the reason?'

He tried to clear the dullness from his mind.

'I ... I had to go home and change my clothes,' he said finally. 'I fell in a puddle.'

It was a ridiculous excuse, and he knew it, but he couldn't think of anything better. And at least it gave him some kind of a reason for not being in school uniform. He heard titters round the class. Mrs Campbell frowned.

'Have you reported to the office?'

'Yes, miss,'

'And where are your books and things?'

'I forgot them.'

She pursed her lips.

'Well, you'd better join us, now you're here, but I'm not very impressed, Jamie. I don't know what's happening to you these days.'

He didn't know either, but there was no point telling Mrs Campbell that. He sat down in his usual place next to Spider and pretended to study the text book his friend had pushed towards him. To his relief, Mrs Campbell turned to the blackboard and started writing. Spider leaned across and whispered.

'Are you OK?'

Jamie stared at him for a moment, then shook his head. Spider leaned closer.

'Mr Talbot came in just after the lesson started and asked if you were here.'

Jamie shrugged. He'd expected the Head to be involved, as Dad's bosom buddy. His father would have rung him first thing this morning at home.

'What did he do when he saw I wasn't here?' he murmured.

'Just went out again.' Spider glanced at Mrs Campbell, who had turned back to the class, and said no more; but Jamie sensed his support.

The lesson dragged on and somehow Jamie managed to stay awake, though he was aching to lower his head to the desk. And he was so hungry now, so desperate for some hot food and a hot drink. Even here, close to the radiator, he felt cold, as though the chill of the shed still clung to him. And the confusion of the night was starting to overwhelm him. He was worrying about Dad, and Mum, and money, and the two men; and now, most of all, the girl.

'Well, Jamie?'

He looked up with a start, realizing Mrs Campbell had asked him a question.

'Yes, miss?'

'The accusative case is for what?'

'The direct object of the sentence,' he said mechanically, just remembering her words a few minutes earlier.

'And the direct object is what?'

He said nothing.

'Jamie? She had that edge back in her voice. 'The direct object is what?'

Luckily Tanya put up a hand.

'Yes, Tanya.'

▷ **6** *whine:* complain in a crying, annoying voice **8** *coincide with sth.:* happen at the same time as sth. **10** *dwell on sth.:*(here) think about sth. too much **19** *clear the dullness from his mind:* make his mind work again **24** *titter* (n): quiet, nervous laughter **30** *purse your lips:* die Lippen schürzen, den Mund spitzen **36** *relief:* Erleichterung **44** *bosom buddy* (infml): very close friend **49** *support* (n): help **50** *drag on:* seem to go on for too long **53** *radiator* ['reɪdieɪtə]: heating device **55** *overwhelm sb.:* jdn. überwältigen **66** *edge:* sharpness

'It's, like, the person or thing that gets something done to it. I mean, like, if the dog bites the man, it's the man that's the object.'

'The direct object, Tanya.'

'Yes, miss.'

Jamie looked at Tanya gratefully and wanted to smile at her; but Mrs Campbell's eyes had fastened upon him again.

'I was hoping you might explain it to us, Jamie. And when else is the accusative case used?'

He didn't know and he didn't care. His thoughts were now fixed on a strange girl who had entered his life and then left it again.

'Jamie?'

'I don't know.'

'Well, perhaps if you'd been paying attention rather than staring out of the window for the last ten minutes, you would know.'

Tanya's hand went up again.

'Yes, Tanya.'

'It's, like, used after certain prepositions.'

'Exactly. And Jamie can copy out the list of them, together with the rest of the section on the accusative case on page 31. Jamie, I'll speak to you afterwards.'

But this was not to be. The door opened and Mr Talbot entered the room.

'Excuse me again, Mrs Campbell. Ah, Jamie, you're here. A word with you in my office, please.'

Jamie stood up, trying to ignore the looks from the rest of the class. He felt a soft pat from Spider as he left the desk and walked over to Mr Talbot. The headmaster led the way down the corridor and didn't speak until they were in his office.

'Sit down, Jamie. Now, what's going on?'

Jamie tried to think of the right thing to say. He knew he couldn't tell Mr Talbot too much, not because he didn't like him or trust him – which he did – but because he knew the headmaster would only see Dad's point of view.

'I had a sort of bust up with my dad,' he said eventually.

'So I gather.' Mr Talbot took his place behind the desk and picked up the phone. 'Ron? It's Jim. Yes, he's here. In my office. Do you want to speak to him? You'll come over. OK, fine. See you in a few minutes. Bye.'

Jamie pictured his father's face and the image frightened him. And he wondered about Mum. Where she was, what she was doing, what she was feeling. Mr Talbot's voice broke in upon him.

'Are you set for the Regional Championships?'

Jamie stared at him. The Regional Championships? As if he cared about the Regional Championships. Strange how Mr Talbot assumed that the boy in front of him was as mad about squash as his father and headmaster were. He tried to drag some kind of response out of himself.

'Yes, sir. I've ... I've been training hard.'

'And how's it going?'

'OK.' He wished they could stop this conversation but the Head was obviously trying to be pleasant.

'Is that other boy going to be playing in the Regionals? What's his name? Ron did mention it. The boy who moved down here last year.'

'Danny Powell.' He remembered Danny punching the air after their last encounter; Bob Powell crowing with jubilation; Dad lashing out in the changing room. He took a slow breath. 'I'm playing him in the first round,' he said.

The Head stroked his chin.

'Danny Powell. That's the one. Good player, I gather. Is he above you in the national rankings?'

'Yes, sir.'

'Well, I'm sure you'll catch him up. I believe he goes to Fairways?'

'Yes, sir.'

Mr Talbot thought for a moment, then chuckled.

'Well, I suppose it's not quite politically correct to say this but I do hope you beat him. It would be so nice to get one over on the public school sector. But don't quote me on that or you'll get me into trouble.'

There was something surreal about all this. Mr Talbot was clearly trying to be friendly and talk about something he thought they were both interested in; yet it was obvious he didn't know whether to be

▷ **1** *like* (adv) (sl): (used when you are thinking what to say) **26** *pat:* soft touch, esp. on sb.'s back **35** *so I gather:* that's what I've heard **42** *be set for*: be prepared for **64** *chuckle* (v): laugh quietly **66** *get one over on sb.* (infml): win against sb. **67** *quote sb. on sth.*: say that sb. said sth. **69** *surreal:* very strange, more like a dream

pleasant to his friend's son or tear him off a strip. He certainly looked as though he'd be glad when Dad turned up.

If so, he was in luck. Jamie could already see the car through the window as it pulled into the school car park. It hadn't taken long; the Head must have contacted Dad on his car-phone. Which meant his father must have been driving around looking for him. Jamie wondered for how long.

Dad climbed out of the car and walked in the main entrance. A moment later there was a knock at the door.

'Come in,' said Mr Talbot.

The Head's secretary appeared.

'Mr Williams is here, headmaster.'

'Thank you, Mrs Beatty.' Mr Talbot stood up. 'Come in, Ron.'

Dad came in and shook hands with Mr Talbot. But his eyes were on Jamie. Jamie shuffled in the chair, wondering how the two men would handle this. How Dad would handle things when they were alone he knew well enough. But for now his father was all smiles.

'Sorry about the inconvenience, Jim. It's just a family misunderstanding. Nothing serious. We'll give Jamie the day off school today – with your agreement – and get him home and shove some food inside him. He looks like he needs it.'

'And a good wash,' said Mr Talbot, also smiling.

So everyone was pretending they were happy. Except him. He could pretend nothing. And even now, in the midst of these charades, he found the face of that girl pressing itself into his mind again.

Dad put an arm round his shoulders.

'Right, Jamie, let's get you home.'

'Keep in touch,' said Mr Talbot.

'No problem.'

Dad led the way out of the office and Jamie followed, wearily, unsure what to make of anything right now. Lack of sleep, lack of food, lack of warmth were nothing to the anguish spreading through his mind. He walked to the car, opened the passenger door and took his place, strangely unconcerned about what he knew was to follow.

'We'll talk later,' Dad said.

And without another word, he started the car and drove them out of the school gate.

Jamie was silent, too, but not now from tiredness or confusion. For in that instant both had vanished. He twisted in his seat and stared as the car sped away.

Standing by the gate, gazing towards the school, were the two men.

▷ **1** *tear sb. off a strip* (infml): speak angily to sb. who has done sth. wrong **16** *handle sth.:* deal with sth. **18** *inconvenience:* trouble **24** *charade* [ʃə'rɑːd]: situation in which people pretend that sth. is true when it is not **32** *anguish* (fml): mental suffering **39** *vanish:* disappear, go away

SEVEN

He sat on his bed, staring out of the window with distaste as drizzle discoloured the morning. Somehow it seemed to match the colour of his thoughts; the colour of his life.

He hated being beaten by his father. It wasn't just the pain, which was always bad, since Dad was a strong man and didn't believe in moderation – it was also the indignity, and the knowledge that he should have the guts to stand up to his father.

Especially as he had not deserved this beating.

He reached behind the bookcase, pulled out his secret book from its hidden place and started writing.

'One day he won't hit me and I'll have a real relationship with him, like Spider does with his dad. I want him to respect me. I know he doesn't respect me. I don't know why. I respect him. And I want to love him but I can't because he won't let me. I know he was a great squash player, better than I'll ever be. I never saw him play but Mum says he was brilliant, and I've read the reports so he must have been good. And he learnt his squash in Australia and Australia is supposed to breed top squash players, so he keeps telling me. But we don't live in Australia.'

He was rambling now and he knew it. He skimmed through the entries he had written over the last few months since he had started keeping the book and found he had written much the same way each time. He was turning into a writing machine; a machine with only one story to tell.

He heard footsteps on the stairs. It would be Mum with tea and toast or some offering. He thrust the book under his pillow. There was a knock at the door.

'Come in,' he called.

Mum entered, as expected with a tray. He watched her, trying to gauge her feelings from the expression on her face, but it was always difficult to know what she was thinking. He wished he could break through the mask of correctness she always seemed to have.

She put the tray on the desk and sat next to him on the bed.

'Jamie –'

'I know. He still loves me. Even though I'm a failure.'

'You're not a failure, darling. And yes, he does love you. Just like I do. You mustn't forget that everything your father says and does is to help you. It's for your own good. No one ever got anywhere without self-discipline. And if someone is struggling to achieve that, he needs someone else to impose that discipline for him. Until he can manage to do it himself.'

Straight out of the manual. It might have been his father speaking or a passage from one of his books. He wished so much that Mum would speak her own mind. But it was always locked behind a façade of perfect behaviour. And despite being knocked about and driven to tears on so many occasions, her loyalty to Dad and her belief that he knew best never seemed to waver.

He took the cup of tea she offered him and sipped at it, unsure what to say. She stiffened suddenly.

'What's that book under your pillow?'

He looked round and saw to his horror the corner of his secret book protruding.

'Oh, it's ... just an exercise book. Something for school.'

'Shouldn't it be in your school bag?'

'Probably, yeah. I'll put it there later.'

She was still looking at it.

'It's a funny place to put an exercise book. Under your pillow.'

▷ **1** *drizzle:* light rain **6** *indignity:* state of feeling of ashamed because you are not treated with respect **7** *guts* (infml): courage **20** *ramble:* talk about sth. in a confused way · *skim through sth.:* look through sth. quickly **26** *thrust sth.:* push sth. quickly **30** *gauge sth.* [geɪdʒ]: make a judgement about sth. (esp. people's feelings) **35** *failure:* person who is not successful **39** *struggle* (v): try hard **40** *impose sth. on sb.:* force sb. to accept sth. difficult or unpleasant **42** *manual* (n): book that tells you how to do or operate sth. **46** *loyalty to sb.* (here): absolute support for sb. **47** *waver* (v): become weak **52** *protrude:* stick out

'Yeah, well, it's –' he pulled the book out as casually as he could, took it over to his school bag and thrust it in. Mum watched him as he came back to the bed.

'You're being a bit secretive,' she said.

He shrugged, trying to think of a way of deflecting further questions. She spoke again.

'I thought maybe you were writing secret letters to a girlfriend.'

It was meant to be a joke, though a slightly probing one. But it gave him a chance to change the subject.

'When have I got time for a girlfriend with all the training he makes me do?'

Sure enough, she immediately forgot the book in the need to defend Dad.

'Jamie, when your father was your age, he had nothing. His parents had had nothing and had to fight for everything they could get. And when they died, it was even worse for him. But he vowed he would never be poor like they had been and he'd only ever be a winner.'

'I've heard this story. You've told me. He's told me.'

A thousand times. A million times.

But she went on, following the script, which he felt he could recite word for word without her. He knew about his father's struggles: parentless at five, brought up by his uncle and aunt in Australia before they dumped him at fifteen to make his own way. And how he fought back, at school, at work; and especially at squash.

'Especially at squash,' he heard Mum say, her lecture keeping pace with his thoughts. 'Think of what he had to do. He was fifteen when he started, not three, like you were. Think of the advantages you've had which he didn't have. And he had to travel miles just to play, and he had to finance himself for it. He couldn't afford more than one trip a week to the courts so he –'

'Painted markings on the walls of an old garage and practised by hitting the ball against them. I know all this.'

'Well, don't be ungrateful, then, and show a little understanding. He's only tough on the world because the world's been tough on him. He's been through a lot. He knows what it's like to fight and he doesn't like to see you throwing your opportunities away.'

After she had gone, he retrieved the secret book from his school bag and replaced it behind the bookcase. Then he sat back on the bed and stared out of the window once more. The allotment was now dull with rain and it was growing cold again.

In the evening the rain stopped. Dad drove him to the school squash court and they did some stroke practice, then went outside to the rugby field for some fitness training. On the way home an idea occurred to him.

After supper he helped Mum with the washing up, while Dad went up to his study to work. At nine o'clock she went in to the sitting room to watch the news.

He waited for a moment to make sure no one was coming back, then grabbed three of the rolls Mum had bought that afternoon, thrust them inside a polythene bag and hurried out of the back door and down to the allotment. The shed loomed before him, dark and silent. He opened the door, cautiously.

There was no one there.

He stole in, left the bag by the old blanket and hurried back to the house.

▷ **1** *casual:* without paying too much attention to what one is doing **4** *secretive* ['siːkrətɪv]: hiding your thoughts, feelings, ideas **5** *deflect sth.:* change the direction of sth. **8** *probing* (adj): intended to discover sth. **16** *vow* (v): make a formal and serious promise **25** *keep pace with sth.*: move at the same speed as sth. **34** *tough* [tʌf]: strict, firm **37** *retrieve sth.*: get sth. back **44** *occur to sb.:* come into sb.'s mind **23** *dump sb./sth.* (infml): get rid of sb./sth. **50** *polythene:* plastic **51** *loom* (v): appear as a large shape

EIGHT

In the morning the rolls were gone. And there was no sign of the girl.

He stared down at the space where they had been, listening all the while for sounds of his parents calling or, worse still, walking down to the shed. But he had chosen his moment carefully, with Dad still shaving and Mum drying after the shower.

He knelt down and checked the blanket. It was flattened where someone – the girl, presumably – had sat on it. He studied it more closely and saw crumbs from the rolls. She must have taken the bag away with her. Then he saw it stuffed behind a plant pot.

He took a slow breath, feeling strangely reassured that she had returned, though he didn't know why. He wondered whether she had been thinking about him as much as he had been thinking about her.

Probably not. She no doubt had far more pressing things to worry about. Just as he had. He hurried back to the house to find Mum already in the kitchen. She looked at him, startled.

'Jamie? Where have you been?'

He had his answer ready. 'I wanted to check the brakes on my bike'

'Aren't they working properly?'

'They felt a bit funny last time I went out.'

'Do you want your father to look at them?'

He shook his head quickly.

'No, there was just something caught in them. They're OK now.'

She hesitated, then spoke again. 'Darling, have you been at the bread bin? I bought some rolls yesterday but some of them seem to have vanished.'

He was ready for this, too.

'Yeah, sorry, I meant to tell you. I was hungry late last night and came down and ate them.' He had a sudden idea. 'They were really nice. Could I take some for lunch today?'

'Of course, darling. How many can you eat?'

'Er ... all of them.'

'There's ten, Jamie. Ten big rolls. I think that's pushing it, even by your standards.'

'No, I could definitely eat ten. I think I need more carbohydrates at the moment. I'm sure that's why I flagged on court the other day.'

He despised himself for this lie; but it didn't work anyway.

'Jamie, you know you're not short of carbohydrates. Your father's been through your diet with you enough times.'

He tried a second lie.

'But I always get hungry about break time and have to go and buy crisps and chocolate and stuff.'

This one worked immediately.

'Jamie!' Mum stared at him. 'I'm horrified. You shouldn't be eating things like that. I had no idea. You'd better not tell your father.' She looked at him, frowning. 'I'll do you seven and we'll see how many you bring back this afternoon.'

'I won't bring any back. I'll eat them all.'

'We'll see about that. What do you want in them? Cheese, salad, peanut butter?'

'Some with cheese, some with salad, please.'

He looked away, uncomfortable at how easy it was to deceive her.

Dad came down, sat at the table without a word and started to read the paper. Jamie glanced at him but there was no response. He frowned. His father had become so much moodier over the last year. Since the squash had started going badly.

Mum hesitated.

'Ron, don't forget the Talbots are coming over for a drink tonight.'

Dad said nothing and simply went on reading the paper.

Jamie looked at her but she turned away, went over to the bread bin and started to prepare the rolls. He sat down at the table and began to

▷ **10** *reassured:* beruhigt **13** *pressing* (adj): urgent, important **25** *vanish:* disappear **34** *carbohydrates:* Kohlehydrate **35** *flag* (v): become tired, weaker **36** *despise sb. for sth.:* dislike and have no respect for sb. **51** *deceive sb.:* make sb. believe sth. that is not true **54** *moody:* launisch

eat. He knew he was out of favour and wouldn't be in favour again until he started winning matches like he used to. But all he wanted to do now was give up squash. He had thought about it a lot.

But somehow he would have to tell his father.

And survive the response.

Mum finished the rolls, packed them up and put them in Jamie's school bag. Jamie watched, forgetting squash now and trying to decide the best way to put his new idea into effect. But he needed to be left alone.

Suddenly Dad pushed his cereal bowl to the side of the table. Mum looked at him.

'There's toast coming.'

'I don't want any.' Dad stood up. 'I've got to get on. Where's that new shirt? I couldn't find it anywhere.'

'In the wardrobe. Hanging up on the left. I did tell you, darling.'

'Well, I couldn't see it.'

'I did put it there.' Mum put the toast on the table in front of Jamie, then looked back at Dad. 'Come on. I bet I'll put my hand straight on it.'

And she led him upstairs.

Jamie waited until they had gone, then jumped to his feet, retrieved the rolls and hurried towards the back door. Then another idea occurred to him.

But he would have to be quick. And very quiet.

He crept to the foot of the stairs and listened. Mum was talking to Dad in the bedroom and he could hear the sound of hangers being pushed along the wardrobe rail. He tiptoed up the stairs as far as the airing cupboard, opened it and took out the big hairy blanket they never used, then slipped back downstairs as quietly as he could.

There was no sound of them returning but they would be back in an instant.

He opened the back door, raced down to the shed with the blanket and rolls, dumped them inside in the corner, and sped back to the house.

Spider kept off awkward questions on the way to school and Jamie was grateful for that. He knew his friend must be buzzing with curiosity about what had happened. But Spider – for all his gentle mockery – could always be trusted not to push things. When he spoke, it was on a safe subject.

'I suppose you're playing squash after school. Or training or something.'

'I'm playing. Dad's picking me up and bringing my kit. So don't hang about for me.'

'Who are you playing? Not that … Danny boy?'

They stopped and looked at each other, and the joke seemed to register with them both at the same time. The next moment they had burst into song.

'Oh, Danny Boy, the pipes, the pipes are calling'

An elderly lady looked quizzically at them from the other side of the road. They broke off, chuckling, and walked on.

'Can't remember the next line,' said Spider.

'Neither can I.'

'So is it this Danny?'

'No, it's Andy Bailey.'

'You said he's good, didn't you?'

'He's not good. He's brilliant.'

'So you're going to get stuffed.'

'That's putting it politely.'

Spider thought for a moment.

'So if you don't mind my asking, what's the point of playing him?'

Jamie looked away. What was the point of playing anyone? He was getting no pleasure from squash now, no matter who the opponent was. He shrugged.

'It's supposed to raise my game.'

'And does it?'

'I don't know.'

They walked on in silence towards the town centre. Suddenly he stopped. Spider looked round at him and stopped, too.

'What's up?'

▷ **1** *be out of / in favour:* (not) be accepted or approved of **28** *airing cupboard* (BE): warm cupboard in which clean sheets, etc. are kept **35** *awkward* ['ɔːkwəd]: (hier) peinlich **36–37** *buzz with curiosity:* vor Neugier platzen **46** *register with sb.:* (here) come to sb.'s attention **48** *Oh, Danny boy …:* first line of a well-known Irish song **49** *quizzical:* showing you are surprised **50** *chuckle* (v): laugh quietly **57** *get stuffed* (BE infml): (here) be totally defeated **64** *raise my game:* improve my way of playing

Jamie nodded forward. It was the two men again, this time approaching down the street. Spider glanced round at them, then back at him.

'What's the problem?'

'Those men. Do you know them?'

'No. Do you?'

'No.'

'So what's the fuss?'

Jamie tried to look casual.

'No fuss.'

Spider shook his head. 'You really are getting paranoid.'

They walked on and the two men drew nearer. Jamie lowered his head but found himself sneaking glances at them even so. Spider stepped to the side to let them pass. But the men stopped and the taller one spoke.

'Excuse me, lads. You got a second?'

It was a high, strangely thin voice, and the accent sounded foreign, though Jamie couldn't place it. He found himself avoiding the eyes of both men. Spider simply looked back at them, confident and unconcerned.

The shorter man pulled something from his pocket.

'Sorry to hold you boys up. I'm sure you're dying to get to school.' He gave a laugh, then held out a photograph. 'Just wondered if you've seen this girl in the area.'

Spider took the photograph, glanced at it and shook his head.

'No.' He held it out to Jamie. 'You seen her?'

Jamie felt his hand tremble as he reached out. The men's eyes, and Spider's, all fixed upon him. He took the photo, knowing what he would see there; and, sure enough, it was her.

He swallowed hard, then shook his head.

'Sorry.'

'Ah, well.' The shorter man took back the photo and smiled. 'Worth a try. We're from a missing persons' bureau and she's been spotted in the area. If you do see anything, can you give this number a call?'

He pulled out a card from his pocket and scribbled a telephone number on it.

'Do two,' said the taller man. 'One for each lad.'

'Don't bother,' said Spider. 'I'll only lose it. Give it to Jamie. He's more organized than I am. If I see anything, I'll get the number from him.'

'Fair enough.' The taller man smiled, then looked at Jamie. 'Think I've seen you around. Haven't you got a house down by the allotments?'

Jamie took the card from the man's companion.

'Yes.'

'Thought so.' The taller man was still smiling, but Jamie had the feeling he was being quietly assessed. 'They're nice houses down there. You've got the one with the basketball ring, right?'

'Yeah.' Jamie shifted from one foot to the other, wishing the men would move on. The taller man looked him over a moment longer, then winked.

'Well, we mustn't hold you two up any longer. Don't want to get you in trouble at school. Thanks for your time.'

And the men moved on.

Spider looked at him.

'What were you so edgy with those men for?'

'I don't know. They just look shifty. Do you reckon they're really from a missing persons' bureau?'

'Why not? People go missing. And other people make a living out of finding them.'

'But those two ... I mean ...' Jamie stopped and examined the card. 'Look, he's just written on a blank card. No name, nothing. If that man was genuine, he'd have had a proper card, you know, with his name and company or whatever. This is just a card with a telephone number. And that's not a local number either.'

Spider glanced at it.

'Probably a mobile phone number. Look, you're worrying about nothing. You haven't seen the girl, so you don't need to have any more

▷ **1** *nod* (v): move your head, usually up or down **8** *fuss* (n): (here) problem **11** *paranoid:* afraid or suspicious of other people and believing that they are trying to harm you **16** *lad* (BE infml): boy **19** *confident:* feeling sure of oneself **27** *tremble:* shake because you are nervous **30** *swallow:* schlucken **33** *worth a try:* einen Versuch wert · *missing person:* person who has disappeared and whose family is trying to find them with the help of the police **34** *spot sb.:* see sb. **48** *assess sb.:* make a judgement about sb. **52** *wink* (v): mit den Augen zwinkern **57** *edgy:* nervous **58** *shifty* (infml): seeming to be dishonest · *reckon* (infml): think **60** *make a living:* earn enough money to buy the things you need in life

contact with those men if you don't like the look of them.' Spider paused. 'You haven't seen the girl, have you?'

Jamie walked quickly on.

''Course I haven't,' he said.

After school, Dad dropped him off at the squash club and drove into Ashingford to buy a new suit. Jamie watched him go, relieved to know that he could disgrace himself on court without worrying about Dad's watchful eye in the gallery above, yet also glad that his father was coming back to give him a lift home. Forty minutes with Andy Bailey were so exhausting they felt like eighty minutes with anybody else.

Yet he liked Andy and was grateful that the older boy was prepared to give up time playing someone he could beat so easily. But halfway through the first game Andy stopped and looked round at him.

'What's bugging you, Jamie? You're playing crap.'

Jamie thought of the two men, and the girl, and his father, and the money, and the almost overwhelming desire to break his racket. But it wasn't fair to burden Andy with his problems.

'I don't know,' he said. 'I just ... can't keep my mind on the game at the moment.'

He heard a booming voice from one of the other courts.

'Come on, Danny, work it, work it!'

Chris Welland. The voice was unmistakable. Danny was going to be even better now that Powell had forked out for the best coach in the area. He saw Andy looking at him.

'Jamie?'

'What?'

'You're a better player than Danny.'

Jamie looked away. 'I don't know about that.'

'I do. He only knows one way to play and he plays it very well but when it doesn't work and he gets into trouble, all he's got left is gamesmanship and arguing with the marker. He'll never go all the way to the top, no matter how much he trains with Welland. Do you know why?'

'Why?'

'Because at heart he's just a bully, like his dad. He likes being aggressive on court and playing people like you who always fold up against him. When you play him, you go into your shell and start playing cautious. You can't do that with Danny. It's like with any other bully, if you go in aggressive and stay aggressive, you'll faze him out. You can't do that against a clever opponent, someone with a bit of court craft, because he'll use your aggression against you. But Danny won't. He hasn't got the tactical sense. He'll go to pieces. Take it from me.'

'How do you know?'

'Because I've done it to him. Lots of times. He never plays me now, except when he has to in a tournament.'

'Yeah, but you're ... I mean ... you're a fantastic player.'

Andy looked at him impatiently.

'So are you, for God's sake. You just forgot it somewhere along the way. Come on. Pretend I'm Danny. Get angry and start treating me like dirt.'

They played on and he felt himself loosen up a little. It was hard to tell whether he was playing better or Andy was just going easy on him. The booming voice from the other court intruded upon his mind as they played out the rallies. But by the end of the game he was feeling a little better.

Though he was well beaten.

And his father was looking down from the gallery.

▷ **6** *relieved:* happy because sth. unpleasant has stopped or not happened **7** *disgrace yourself:* behave in a way that makes you or other people feel ashamed **10** *exhausting:* making you feel very tired **14** *bug sb.* (infml): annoy or irritate sb. · *crap* (BE slang): (here) bad(ly) **16** *overwhelming* [ˌəʊvəˈwelmɪŋ]: very strong **23** *fork out for sb./sth.* (infml): spend a lot of money to get sb./sth. **31** *marker:* referee **35** *bully:* person who gains power over weaker people by cruelty **36** *fold up* (infml): give in **39–40** *faze sb. out* (infml): make sb. feel confused or shocked **41** *court craft:* (here) tactical knowledge and skill in the court **53** *go easy on sb.* (infml): treat sb. in a gentle way **54** *intrude upon sth.:* disturb or have an unpleasant effect on sth.

NINE

He wasn't sure what to think that evening when the Talbots turned up for a drink. He'd always been uncomfortable about Dad's friendship with the Head. Somehow it made him feel he was always under Dad's eyes, even at school, and that whatever he did there would somehow get back.

And for the Talbots to come round on a Tuesday was unusual. They often came for dinner or a drink, but it was generally at the weekend. He couldn't imagine they wanted to talk school business. It was more likely to be squash.

And so it proved.

The conversation ranged from tournament to tournament, player to player, match to match, and inevitably to him. He looked round and imagined for a moment the effect if he chose this precise time to announce his desire to give up the game. And for a crazy moment it seemed almost a good idea. Dad couldn't possibly hit him in front of all these people.

But the reaction later would be terrible; more so for the public embarrassment caused. No, this was not the moment. And besides, he had another thing on his mind. He fumbled for an excuse to leave the room.

Fortunately there was one that none of them could disapprove of.

'I've got some homework to get on with.'

'Good lad,' said Mr Talbot. 'Nice to see you back in school today, by the way.'

Jamie nodded at him uneasily. Then he saw Mrs Talbot smiling at him.

'What is it tonight, Jamie? Maths? French?'

'English. We've got an essay on Macbeth.'

She raised an eyebrow.

'And very appropriate on a dark, chilly night like this. Ideal conditions for meeting witches on the heath.'

'Except there isn't a heath,' said Mr Talbot.

She shrugged.

'Well, the allotment out the back's a bit on the wild side. With a little poetic licence, you could almost imagine meeting strange people there. I'm sure Jamie knows what I mean.'

He smiled at her, warily, unsure whether anything lay behind her words. But it was unlikely. She was too direct. He'd always liked Mrs Talbot. Dad laughed.

'I know we've neglected the allotment but I think describing it as a meeting-place for witches is a bit excessive.'

The others chuckled. Dad turned to Jamie.

'All right, lad, off you go.'

He left the room gratefully and hurried upstairs. He had done what he could of the Macbeth essay during the lunch hour, mostly with Spider's help, since he hadn't read the scenes he was supposed to have studied. It wasn't a good essay but he didn't care. He was only interested in one thing right now.

He gazed out of his bedroom window towards the allotment.

It was hard to see anything clearly so he turned off the light, opened the window and stared again, waiting for his eyes to grow used to the darkness.

Gradually the outline of the sheds came to him, then their own, slightly apart from the rest. The door was closed and there was nothing to indicate whether anyone was or had been there. He stayed by the window, watching, despite the chill of the night that now seeped in through the window.

▷ **1** *turn up:* come unexpectedly **10** *so it proved:* that was what happened **12** *inevitably:* unausweichlich **18** *embarrassment:* awkward or guilty feeling **19** *fumble for sth.:* have difficulty finding sth. **24** *by the way:* übrigens **30** *appropriate:* suitable **32** *heath:* Heide (in Shakespeare's play *Macbeth*, Macbeth meets three witches on the heath who tell him about his future) **35** *poetic licence:* dichterische Freiheit **38** *unlikely:* unwahrscheinlich **41** *excessive:* exaggerated, going too far **53** *gradually:* slowly **57** *seep in:* (here) come slowly through very small openings

Downstairs he heard the Talbots laughing, and Dad offering more drinks. And he suddenly realized how quiet Mum was. She had said little while he was with them and since he had come upstairs, he had hardly heard her voice at all. There was a strange remoteness about her.

The Talbots didn't stay late and when Mum and Dad looked in on their way to bed, he was ready at his desk with books spread all around him.

'I thought you'd be changed for bed,' said Mum.

'I've been busy with the essay.'

He looked at her, trying to gauge what was wrong. She came over and kissed him.

'I think it's time to sleep now, darling. You must have finished it, surely.'

'Yes, I was just going to get undressed.'

'All right. Goodnight, darling.'

'Goodnight.'

She left the room but Dad remained in the doorway. His face looked a little florid as though he had drunk more than usual. He nodded to Jamie.

'Difficult essay?'

'Yes.'

'But you managed it all right.'

'Yes.'

'Good.'

And his father turned and left.

Jamie undid his shirt to make it look as though he were getting undressed, then sat on the bed and waited. Fortunately, they didn't take long in the bathroom and he soon heard the click of their door, then silence.

He left it a good while to make sure, then fastened his shirt buttons again and pulled on his thick pullover. Then he slipped out on to the landing as quietly as he could and listened.

There was no sound from his parents' room so he crept downstairs to the hall, took his coat from the peg and the torch from the cabinet, and stole through to the kitchen.

This was the first risky part, but he had decided it was essential. He filled the kettle, switched it on, then listened again. But the house remained silent and there was no sound of movement upstairs. He left the lights off and stood there in the darkness, staring at the little power-light on the kettle as the water heated up.

Still there were no sounds from upstairs. He fetched the big thermos flask from the bottom cupboard, washed it out and spooned in some coffee granules, and a little sugar.

The sound of the kettle seemed horribly loud now and he was sure his parents must hear it, even with the door shut. But still there were no voices, no footsteps on the stairs.

The kettle switched itself off with a loud click, then silence fell once more.

He listened again, then poured the hot water into the thermos, added a little milk, and screwed on the top. Then he glanced around the kitchen.

Mum had bought some more rolls but he didn't dare take any this time. He hunted round, opening cupbards, looking in the fridge, and before long had a carrier bag stuffed with pieces of cake, slices of bread, apples, bananas, a bar of chocolate, and some crisps.

He tiptoed to the back door, opened it as softly as he could, and crept out into the night.

There was a deep stillness around him, though now and then he heard the drone of cars from the town centre. He clutched the bag to him, slipped down to the gate at the bottom of the garden, and made his way down to the allotment.

The sheds rose about him like dusky fingers pointing at the sky. He found he was shivering already, and very nervous. Suddenly he stopped.

A light was approaching from the far end of the allotment, a small moving beam from a torch darting across the ground. It was a couple of hundred yards away but drawing closer even as he watched. He slid behind the nearest shed and waited, trying to decide what to do.

He could nip back to the house. or just walk back. After all, he wasn't doing anything wrong. But whoever was coming would probably be near enough now to see him, and which house he went into.

▷ **4** *remoteness:* distance, feeling of isolation **19** *florid:* red **33** *landing:* area at the top of a staircase **35** *peg:* hook for hanging coats, etc. · *torch:* Taschenlampe **36** *steal - stole - stolen:* move secretly and quietly **38** *kettle:* Wasserkocher **60** *drone* (n): continuous low noise · *clutch sth.:* hold sth. tightly **67** *beam:* Strahl **70** *nip back to sth.* (infml): go to sth. quickly

He clenched his hand tight round the handle of the bag. It shouldn't matter, he told himself. He wasn't doing anything illegal. He had every right to be out here. There was no reason why he shouldn't just walk back to the house.

But he did not move. He knew he could not.

The light vanished behind one of the sheds and he heard the sound of someone trying the door. Then the light reappeared, flickering around the top end of the allotment as it lit up the dark soil before vanishing again. It was drawing closer. Soon it would be upon him.

There was no hiding place here. He pressed himself against the wall of the shed, tensed, ready to run. He wondered about the girl. Somehow he had dismissed from his mind the possibility that this could be her. He did not remember her having a torch and, even if she had one, he felt sure she would not use it now. She had been here before, and she wouldn't want to draw attention to herself. It was more likely to be the two men. Or someone else.

He heard footsteps, then the sound of another door being tried, one of the smaller sheds up to the left. Then more footsteps. The beam flashed to his right and he heard another door being tried, still not his shed, but they were close now. They would try his one soon. He prayed that the girl would not be here. But even if they didn't find her here, they would surely see the blanket and know someone had been there.

They.

He wondered why he assumed it was more than one person. He had seen nobody, only the torchlight. But he sensed it was the two men.

Suddenly, about thirty yards away, two figures appeared. They were walking to the left of him to check the sheds up by the houses, and he saw them for a moment before they disappeared from view.

It was them. There was no doubt about it. But there was no time to ponder this. The beam was already approaching as they made their way down towards his parents' shed. After that they would check here.

Unless they found the girl first.

He clenched his fists. He couldn't stay here but he also knew he couldn't abandon her. If she were in the shed and they found her, he would have to do something. The light flashed upon his parents' shed; then he heard the door open and they went in.

He waited, listening for words, or sounds of violence. There were none.

But he heard them rummaging about.

He knew it was now or never. In a trice he was hurrying back towards the house, expecting the beam to fall over him any second, or a voice to call out. But nothing checked him. A moment later he was behind the gate, holding it just open so he could peep through the gap.

The figures came out and lingered by the shed, talking in low voices. It was obvious they hadn't found her, but they would have seen the blanket and the cushion. He wondered what they would do next.

To his relief, they seemed to be leaving. Presumably they were satisfied with what they had found, or had just had enough. They didn't bother to look at the remaining sheds. He watched them go and even stepped out of the gate again to watch their forms disappear completely from view.

He looked down at the bag he had packed for the girl and wondered what to do with it. It would certainly be risky taking it down there now. The shed was not a safe place for her and the last thing he wanted to do was encourage her to come back here.

He decided to leave her a note. He would go back to the kitchen, write her an anonymous warning note and leave it in the shed, in case she returned.

But there was no time for that.

At the far end of the allotment a new figure had appeared.

▷ **1** *clench sth.:* press sth. tightly · *handle:* Griff **11** *tensed:* gespannt **12** *dismiss sth. from your mind:* put sth. out of your mind **32** *ponder sth.:* think about sth. carefully **37** *abandon sb.:* leave sb. **42** *rummage about:* move things around carelessly while searching for sth. **43** *in a trice:* very quickly or suddenly **48** *linger* ['lɪŋgə]: spend a long time doing sth. **52** *to his relief:* zu seiner Erleichterung **54** *remaining* (adj): which have not yet been dealt with or looked at

TEN

He slipped back inside the gate and watched again, keeping as still as he could. It was hard to see the face of this new person and there was now no torchlight to give him a clue. But it had to be the girl. How many more people could there be, wandering about this place in the chill of night?

But if it were the girl, she was surely in danger, and he must tell her so.

He continued to watch. The figure reached the shed, opened the door and disappeared inside.

It had to be her. He clutched the bag to himself and made his way down towards the shed. A few feet away he stopped and looked about him for signs of the men. There were none. He tiptoed up to the door, eased it a fraction ajar and peered through.

Suddenly it flew open.

The edge drove into his face with a thud. He jumped back, momentarily blinded, and dropped the bag to the ground. The next moment, he felt hands clawing at his eyes.

'Get off!' he muttered, twisting his face away.

A knee drove into his groin.

'Ah!' He doubled up but somehow managed to stumble a few steps away from the shed. But his attacker had drawn back.

He turned, feeling his groin gingerly, and stared towards the shed.

The girl was standing there, watching him. She seemed ill-at-ease, as though unsure how to react to him. But after a while she spoke.

'Sorry.'

She glanced down at the bag he had dropped. He took a step forward – then stopped, seeing her stiffen.

'It's for you,' he said. 'I brought it in case you needed it.'

She reached awkwardly down and picked it up, keeping her eyes on him as though she still didn't fully trust him. Then she glanced inside it.

'You brought this for me?'

'Yeah.'

She thought for a moment. 'Did you leave those rolls, too?'

'Yeah.'

She stared at him for a moment.

'Thanks,' she said eventually. She glanced round the allotment. 'I thought you were somebody else.'

'I know.' He saw a questioning look on her face and went on. 'There's two men looking for you. They're asking questions. They stopped me and my friend in the street today and showed us your photo.' He saw the alarm on her face and quickly added: 'It's OK. I said I hadn't seen you.'

'Does your friend know about me?'

'No. I haven't told anyone about you.' He paused. 'The men said they were from a missing persons' agency.'

She said nothing but he noticed the scorn in her face.

'They were here a few minutes ago,' he said. 'I came out to leave this stuff for you and nearly got caught by them. They were looking in the sheds. They'll have seen the blanket and cushion.' He studied her face. 'Are you all right?'

She had started breathing heavily and had a hand on her stomach.

He took a step forward. 'Is it … I mean, can I …?'

But she waved him away, struggled with the bag back to the shed and disappeared inside, without closing the door. He stood there, unsure what to do. She was clearly not well and the exertion of fighting him couldn't have helped.

▷ **3** *clue:* idea, hint **13** *ease sth.:* move sth. slowly and carefully · *fraction:* very small amount · *ajar:* a little bit open **15** *thud:* sound made when a heavy object hits sth. else **17** *claw at sth.:* scratch or tear sth. with your fingernails **19** *groin:* Leiste **20** *double up:* sich krümmen **22** *gingerly* ['dʒɪndʒəli]: in a careful way because you are afraid of being hurt **23** *ill-at-ease:* uncomfortable and embarrassed **27** *stiffen:* become firm and straight due to fear, etc. **47** *scorn:* Verachtung **54** *struggle with sth.:* move sth. with difficulty **56** *exertion:* physical effort

Perhaps he should just leave her now. He had given her the food and the coffee, warned her about the men. She hadn't asked him to hang around.

He stared at the open door of the shed, then slowly walked over to it and looked in.

She was slumped against the wall in the corner on the thick hairy blanket he had left here earlier, the cushion stuffed behind her back. And she was eating.

Ravenously.

Never in his life had he seen anyone eat that way. She attacked the food like a starving dog, biting off chunks and swallowing almost without chewing.

He wished now that he had brought more. He stayed by the entrance, unsure whether to come in and sit down. She took no notice of him at first and seemed intent only on the food; then she glanced up at him.

'You'd better close the door if those men are around.'

He did as she said and darkness fell upon them. But he saw her form huddled in the corner as she went on devouring the food. She had not touched the coffee yet. All she wanted was bulk. He wondered again whether he should go.

Then she moved.

It was only a small thing, just a shift of her body to the side and a glance towards him, before she turned back to the food. But it was enough for him to recognize an invitation.

He hesitated, then stepped forward and sat down next to her. The under-blanket had moved to the side with her, and he felt only the damp boards of the shed against his trousers, but she seemed aware of this and stopped eating again to pull the blanket back for him. Then, without a word, she draped the other blankets over their legs.

'Thanks,' he said.

She said nothing and continued attacking the food.

He leaned back against the wall of the shed, thinking about Dad and Mum, and squash, and all that was wrong with his life. It didn't seem sensible to get mixed up in this girl's life, especially with those men involved.

He stole a glance at her in the darkness and saw she had finished the food and was unscrewing the thermos flask. Suddenly she turned to him.

'Why are you doing all this for me?'

He felt the intensity in her eyes and wanted to look away.

'I don't know. I just –'

'I can't give you anything back.' She gave him a defiant look. 'I won't give you anything back So if you're expecting –'

'I'm not expecting anything. I don't want anything from you.'

They stared at each other in the darkness. After a moment she looked away, poured some coffee from the flask and took a sip; then, to his surprise, offered the cup to him.

He thought for a moment, wondering whether to refuse and show her he had some pride of his own; but he was thirsty, and perhaps it would be good to share something small between them. He took the cup, blew on the coffee and sipped a little, then handed it back.

'You drink the rest. I can have as much coffee as I like. I only live a few yards away.'

She gave a start. 'Which house?'

He frowned. He hadn't intended to tell her where he lived. But now that he'd blurted this much out, he might as well tell her the rest.

'The one with the big brown gate at the bottom and –'

'The basketball ring.'

'Yes.'

She looked slightly sheepish for a moment, then reached into a pocket and thrust some coins into his hand.

'It's all I've got left.'

He stared at her. 'What's this for?'

'It's from your house. I'm sorry. I wouldn't have taken it if I'd known you were going to help me. But your mother left the back door unlocked and her handbag in view of the window so what did she expect?'

He looked away, unsure what to say.

'I didn't take anything else,' she said.

▷ **6** *be slumped:* sit with your body leaning forward **9** *ravenous* ['rævənəs]: (here) quickly because one is so hungry **19** *huddle:* hold your arms and legs close to your body usually because you are cold or frightened · *devour sth.:* eat all of sth. quickly **20** *bulk:* solid things **28** *damp:* not quite dry **35** *sensible:* vernünftig **43** *defiant* [dɪ'faɪənt]: aufsässig **56** *frown* (v): die Stirn runzeln **57** *blurt sth. out:* say sth. quickly without thinking **61** *sheepish:* embarrassed, ashamed

There was something in her voice, something more conciliatory than before, as though she felt she owed him something now – but not too much. They sat in silence for a few minutes, the girl sipping more coffee. Then she spoke again.

'How long are you staying here for?'

'I don't know. I suppose –'

'Only it's getting cold and if you're staying, we'd better lie together again.'

He detected the tension in her voice and quickly tried to reassure her.

'It's OK. You can have the blankets to yourself. I won't be stopping. I'll go back to the house in a minute. But I'm still worried about you out here on your own. Those men might come back tonight. They –'

He stopped, aware that she was watching him intently. Then she spoke.

'Don't get mixed up in my life.'

It didn't sound like a threat; more like a warning. He sensed she wanted him to drop the subject. But he knew he could not.

'So what are you going to do tomorrow night? It'll be risky coming back here. Even if the men don't come back tonight, they're bound to come back some time soon.'

'You don't need to bother about that. I can take care of myself.'

'But you need somewhere to go.'

'I told you. You don't need to bother. I'll look after myself.'

There was a finality in her voice that told him it was time to shut up. And he knew he should. This was, after all, her business. But he had had an idea and, at the risk of annoying her, he knew he had to express it.

'Listen, I don't want to interfere – OK? – but if you get stuck tomorrow night and you need a place to doss down, I could probably find you somewhere. Not here, I mean. Somewhere else where you should be safe for the night.'

She said nothing and it was hard to tell whether she was angry with him or not. He waited for a moment, then, with a slight hesitation, handed her back the money.

'Keep this. And just leave the thermos flask and stuff here. I'll pick them up in the morning. And if you ... I mean ... if you do need somewhere, meet me tomorrow night about half twelve in the town centre. Next to the health food shop there's a small alleyway. People often park motorbikes in there. It doesn't lead very far and –'

'I know it.' The voice was flat; neither approving nor disapproving.

'Well, I'll come down about half twelve. Or it might be later. It depends when my parents go to bed. But they usually go to bed early and I can –'

'There's no point in coming. I won't be there.'

Her voice was sharper this time and he knew he had said enough. He saw her face soften slightly, as though she felt she needed to offer him something. She spoke again.

'I know you mean well. But I told you, don't get involved in my life.'

He absolutely must go now. She was trying to be kind to him, in a strange, bruising kind of way and he shouldn't try to push things further. He stood up and, against all his reasoning, added one last thing.

'It's no problem if you've got somewhere else to go. But I'll be there about twelve-thirty just in case. And I'll bring more food.'

And before she could answer, he stepped out of the shed and hurried back to the house.

▷ **1** *conciliatory* [kən'sɪliətəri]: versöhnlich **2** *owe sb. sth.:* jdm. etwas schuldig sein **18** *threat* [θret]: Drohung **19** *drop a subject:* stop talking about sth. **23** *bother about sth.:* spend time and/or energy doing sth. **30** *interfere:* get involved in and try to influence a situation that does not concern you · *get stuck:* (here) not know what to do in a particular situation **31** *doss down* (sl) : sleep in an unauthorised place **42** *(dis)approving:* showing that you believe sth. is (not) good **53** *bruising:* making you feel hurt

ELEVEN

It was at breakfast that he knew for certain something was wrong with Mum.

She would not meet his eyes.

He sat at the table, asking himself whether lack of sleep made him see things that weren't there. She had spoken to him willingly enough, albeit about mundane things like sandwiches for school and what he wanted for breakfast. He glanced at her again and tried to catch her eye.

She looked away once more.

Dad seemed to notice none of this and simply read the paper in silence. Jamie started his cereal, feeling more and more anxious. Maybe Mum and Dad had had a row and Dad had hit her again.

No, this was something different. He sensed it. It was between Mum and himself.

Dad stirred suddenly and glanced across at him.

'I might be a few minutes late picking you up for the gym this afternoon. I've got to go into Ashingford. Just wait by the school gate.'

'OK.'

Dad was silent for a moment but Jamie knew something was waiting to be said; and finally it came.

'I want much more effort from you with the weights, Jamie. Most of your problems are down to your poor mental attitude in matches, but I've noticed your fitness levels aren't what they should be either. I want to see something good from you this afternoon.'

Jamie frowned. He hated weight training, especially as he sometimes bumped into Danny and Bob Powell at the gym. And he did try hard.

'I do my best,' he said eventually, his mind still on Mum as she stood at the cooker. Dad shook his head.

'Your best'll have to be far better than what I'm seeing. You just don't push yourself. You'll really have to sharpen up if you're going to get past Danny in the Regionals.'

Mum was hovering by the table, ready to take away Dad's bowl. Jamie looked straight at her and tried again to catch her eye. She looked at him this time, somewhat warily, and seemed to be trying to smile. Then her eyes moved away. Dad handed her his bowl; she took it over to the sink, then returned to the table and put a plate of scrambled eggs in front of him.

'Jamie?' she said. 'Scrambled eggs for you?'

Her voice sounded as though it would break any moment.

'Yes, please,' he said. 'Mum, are you –?'

'Do you want some mushrooms with them?'

'Er … yes, please.'

She turned quickly back to the cooker. Dad swivelled round in his chair to look at her.

'I thought you were doing me some mushrooms.'

She whirled round. 'Oh, darling, I'm sorry. I forgot. I'll do them now.'

'No, leave it. I haven't got time.'

'I'm sorry, darling. I just …'

Her sentence trailed away. Dad said no more and ate his scrambled eggs. Jamie sat watching Mum cook, wondering whether to try and speak to her again. But she clearly did not want to talk. She put his own scrambled eggs in front of him. There were no mushrooms for him either. But he said nothing.

Dad finished his breakfast and left the room. Jamie glanced at Mum again. She was standing by the sink, her back towards him.

'Mum,' he said, 'is there –?'

'Can you pass me your plate, darling?'

He stood up, took his plate and walked slowly over to her. Perhaps he should force this. Make her give him a direct answer. But if she really didn't want to talk, it didn't seem right. He held out his plate.

▷ **6** *albeit* [ˌɔːlˈbiːɪt] (fml): although · *mundane:* not interesting or exciting **12** *row* [raʊ] (n): fight **13** *sense sth.:* feel sth. **31** *sharpen up:* become better or more skilful **33** *hover by sth.* [ˈhɒvə]: stay close to sth. without any real reason **37** *sink:* Spülbecken **51** *trail away:* become gradually less and then disappear

'Mum ...'

But she merely took the plate from him and turned back to the sink.

'You'd better hurry up, darling. You'll be late for school.'

Spider was beaming as they walked to school.

'Call me genius. I've found it.'

'Found what?'

'Wake up. What's the one thing I've been looking for lately?'

'Even more girlfriends than you've already got?'

'My dream car, thicko. Dad's found a guy at work who's got exactly the one I want. Even the right colour. His wife's decided he looks stupid in a young man's car and says it's too thirsty on juice.'

'It will be when you start driving it.'

'It's not absolutely settled. I haven't paid anything yet. We had a look at it last night but didn't have time for a spin 'cause Dad had a meeting at the bridge club, so we just checked the engine over and hunted for rust and things like that. Couldn't find a thing wrong. The man's a fanatic. I reckon he's spent more time cleaning it than driving it. I suppose I'll have to do the same until I'm seventeen. Still, I can live with that.'

Spider's face was flushed with pleasure. Jamie felt happy for him. At least one of them had something to celebrate. Spider glanced round.

'No sign today, then.'

'No sign of what?'

'Those two men asking about the missing girl.'

'Oh.' Jamie tried not to sound interested, though his eyes had been searching for them, too.

'Wonder if they found her,' said Spider.

'Don't suppose we'll ever know.'

'I tell you what, I think you're right. There's no way they're from a missing persons' agency. I wonder who they are.'

Jamie looked away. He didn't want to know who they were. And he certainly didn't want to see them again.

But he did see them again. Straight after school.

They were sauntering up the lane towards the school gate where he stood, waiting for Dad to arrive to take him to the gym. He pulled the hood up on his jacket to conceal his face and turned to look into the playground. A girls' netball match was in progress and he watched it, keeping his back to the lane and hoping the men would pass without noticing him.

'Jamie!'

He turned reluctantly and saw them standing a few feet away. The taller man was smiling at him.

'Thought it was you.'

Jamie looked at him suspiciously. 'How do you know my name?'

'Your friend mentioned it when we met you in the street.'

'Oh.'

'So, how are you? Cold, obviously.'

'What?

'You've got your hood up.' The man still smiled. 'And I was just saying to my friend here that I thought today was slightly warmer than yesterday. Still chilly, though, isn't it? Too cold to be hanging around. Waiting for your mate?'

'No.'

He didn't see why he should tell them what he was doing. The shorter man's eyes wandered over to the playground and rested on the netball players for a moment, then fixed on Jamie again.

'No sign of our girl, then?' He made to produce the photograph but Jamie waved it away.

'I don't need to see it. I can remember it.'

'So have you seen her?'

'No.'

The man's eyes seemed to search his for a few moments. There was something chilling about both men but this shorter man seemed somehow even more frightening. The taller man spoke.

'Jamie, if you see anything or know anything, you will get in touch with us, won't you? It's urgent. We're very worried about her. We know she's in the area. She's been seen by several people.'

▷ **5** *beam* (v): have a big happy smile on your face **10** *thicko* (sl): stupid person **12** *be too thirsty on juice* (infml): use too much petrol **15** *spin* (n) (infml): short ride in a car **36** *saunter* ['sɔːntə]: walk in a slow, relaxed way **38** *hood:* Kapuze · *conceal sth.:* hide sth. **43** *reluctant:* waiting before doing sth. because you do not want to do it **46** *suspicious:* (here) fearing danger; not trusting sb. **54** *mate* (BE, infml): friend **59** *make to do sth.* (infml): start to do sth.

'What's she done?' he said, and cursed himself at once. The more he showed interest, the more they would hang around and maybe even suspect he knew something. He mustn't give them any clues. But the question had been asked.

The taller man answered it.

'You'll appreciate, Jamie, we can't divulge any precise information. We're bound by confidentiality. But we can tell you she's in danger. If you do know where she might be, or if you've seen her somewhere, you'll be doing her a favour by letting us know. And you'll be doing yourself a favour. There's money in it for you.'

Both men were watching him keenly now. The shouts of the girls in the playground, the sound of the whistle, all seemed suddenly distant. Pupils were still coming out of the school and he saw faces turn towards him and the two men. But the men's eyes remained on him.

'I haven't seen her,' he said finally.

Still they watched him, and he had the feeling they suspected he was lying. Then the taller man smiled.

'Well, I'll give you our telephone number again. I expect you've lost the card we gave you.' He reached into his pocket.

'Don't bother. I've still got it.'

The man checked himself, then smiled again. 'All right, Jamie. We'll see you around.'

And they walked on up the lane.

Jamie watched them go, feeling more uneasy about them than ever. A few moments later a car horn sounded behind him.

It was Dad.

Jamie frowned as the problem of the men faded and the problem of squash returned.

TWELVE

Somehow he had to tell his father, no matter what it cost.

He climbed in the car, clipped on the safety belt and went over in his head the things he had to say. Dad turned the car in the lane and drove back to the main road.

'Dad ...' he began.

'Damn!' His father scowled as they locked into a traffic queue. 'We should have gone the other way.'

Jamie said nothing for a few moments, then nodded ahead.

'It's moving.'

Dad eased the car forward a few yards before they had to stop again.

'We'll never get there at this rate.' He looked round suddenly. 'Well?'

'Well what?'

'What happened at school today?'

'Just lessons.'

'What lessons?'

'Science, German, English, Maths.'

'And?'

'And what?'

▷ **1** *curse yourself:* (here) be angry with yourself **6** *appreciate sth.:* (here) understand and accept sth. · *divulge sth. to sb.:* give sb. sth. (esp. information that is supposed to be secret) **7** *be bound by confidentiality:* be expected to keep information secret **28** *fade:* disappear gradually **35** *scowl:* speak or look in an angry or annoyed way **41** *at this rate:* (here) at this speed **47** *science:* biology, chemistry and physics

'And how did they go?'

'OK.'

The traffic started moving again. Dad drove on, saying nothing, and Jamie sat there, silent too, aware that yet again he could not bring himself to confront his father over squash.

Ten minutes later they were at the gym.

Jamie didn't like the gym but he did like its owner.

Greg Mason was in his early thirties and dedicated to physical fitness, but he was also his own man and didn't kowtow to anyone. His gym was popular and the numbers of men in particular were increasing, especially since the appointment of Stephanie for physiotherapy and massage.

But Greg was far more than just a meat-loaf pumping iron. He'd had a great deal to do with Andy's startlingly improved level of fitness this season, and now he was helping Danny on a regular basis, which, Jamie thought, was probably the reason why Dad had now taken over his own weight-training programme.

Whatever the reason, it was no coincidence that Jamie's gym sessions were scheduled at different times to Danny's. It was rare for them to meet here.

But today was to be one of those occasions. To his dismay, he found Danny and Bob standing in the entrance, talking to Greg. Dad nodded to Powell and they exchanged the briskest of courtesies.

'Bob.'

'Ron.'

Greg was not favoured with a word of greeting, but Dad always acted strangely with people who weren't intimidated by him. Jamie caught Danny's eye. Neither spoke.

Dad turned round.

'Right, Jamie. Go and get changed.'

He hurried to the changing room, glad to be free of the tension for a moment, but Danny soon appeared, and the two boys started changing. He wondered whether he should try and say something. But Danny did not speak and, as the minutes passed, the silence seemed only to deepen.

Danny finished changing first and walked through to the weights room. Jamie took his time, glad to be alone for a moment, then, unable to put things off any longer, made his way through as well.

Surprisingly, there were no other members there. Dad was standing stiffly to one side of the room, Powell equally stiffly on the other. He went through the warm up, secretly watching Danny doing the same, then made his way over to the exercise bike. Danny was already astride the other bike but hadn't started yet as Greg was adjusting the settings.

Dad came over.

'Right, Jamie. On you go.'

Jamie climbed on the bike and glanced to his right. But Danny was staring straight ahead. Greg straightened up and looked at Danny.

'Right, try it on that setting but don't push it. It's more than you've been doing. If you find it a struggle, put it back on the old setting.'

'OK,' said Danny.

'Good boy. How are you doing, Jamie?'

'Fine.' Jamie wished the others would go away and leave him to train in peace. And he wished Danny weren't here. He started to adjust the setting on his own bike.

But Dad leaned forward. 'I'll do it.'

Jamie gasped as he saw his father raise the setting to the same level as Danny's.

He looked away, unsure what to do. Greg would have prepared Danny for this setting but Jamie wasn't ready for it, and he knew it. Ever since Dad had discarded Greg's services and taken over the weight training himself, things had been far less systematic.

He had to resist this. But now here was Powell getting involved.

'Right, boys. Let's see who's got the gas!'

Danny made to start pedalling and instinctively Jamie found himself doing the same. But Greg reached out a hand to each of them and they stopped.

▷ **8** *dedicated to sth.:* working hard at sth. because you think it is good **9** *be your own man:* act and think independently · *kowtow to sb.* (infml): show sb. in authority too much respect and be too willing to obey them **13** *meat-loaf:* Muskelprotz · *pump iron* (infml): lift heavy weights in order to strengthen your muscles **21** *dismay* (n): worried feeling after you have received an unpleasant surprise **23** *brisk:* quick · *courtesy:* polite thing you say or do when you meet people **27** *intimidate sb.:* frighten or threaten sb. so that they will do what you want **43** *astride:* with one leg on each side of sth. **44** *setting:* (here) position at which the controls for speed, etc. on a machine can be set **61** *discard sb./sth.:* get rid of sb./sth. that you no longer want or need **63** *resist sth.* [rɪˈzɪst]: refuse to accept sth. and try to stop it from happening

'You,' he said, looking at Danny, 'are here to train, not compete.' He turned to Powell. 'And you're here to watch, not egg him on. Save the rivalry for the squash court.' His eyes fixed on Jamie. 'And you're not ready for this setting.' He leaned across to adjust it.

Dad reached forward and stopped him.

'Leave it. He's managed that setting before. He's used to it.'

'He's not ready.'

'He is. Ask him yourself.'

Jamie felt Greg's eyes burn into him. But his father's eyes burned deeper still. And in spite of himself, the answer stuttered out.

'It's ... it's fine. I'm ... I'm OK with it.'

Greg looked at him hard.

'Jamie, people who come to my gym do things right or they don't do them at all. They're out.' He paused. 'You can try that setting for a bit, but if it's too much, you stop and lower it. Is that clear?

'Yes.'

Dad tapped Greg on the shoulder.

'I told you. He's fine on this setting. There's no need to interfere. We know what we're doing.'

Greg looked round.

'If someone's doing something wrong in my gym, I'll tell them about it. If they take no notice, then they're out. Simple as that. I don't have room for lawsuits with people who hurt themselves because they ignore my advice.'

Dad stiffened. 'Jamie's training under my direction. Any mistakes will be my responsibility.'

Greg narrowed his eyes. 'They certainly will be.'

He nodded to Jamie and Danny. 'I'll be keeping an eye on the pair of you.' He glanced at Dad and Powell, and Jamie sensed that the words applied just as much to them.

Stephanie appeared at the door. 'Greg. Phone.'

'All right. I'm coming.'

And, with a last look round, he hurried out.

'Thank God for that,' muttered Dad.

Powell looked at him and Jamie detected an ominous agreement between them, though no words were spoken. Dad turned back to Jamie.

'Right, get started.' Then he leaned forward and whispered. 'And I don't want Danny upstaging you. You don't stop before he does. Understand?'

Jamie stared down at the floor, wishing he could climb off and run away from all this. But he heard Danny start pedalling and before he knew what was happening, he was pedalling, too.

At once he felt the resistance of the higher setting and he knew at once that he would not be able to keep going long. Danny was driving the pedals hard, and as Jamie struggled to do the same, he became aware of Powell and his father moving closer.

Watching.

Soon the strain in his legs was starting to tell. He lowered his head and forced himself to drive his legs down, down, down. Already he yearned to stop, and they had only been going a short time.

Danny must be hurting, too. He surely couldn't keep this up either. But the whirr of the pedals went on next to him. Then the talking started. Dad first.

'Come on, boy, don't ease up.'

And Powell.

'Go on. Danny, go on.'

Jamie scowled at the two men. They just couldn't resist, despite what Greg had said. He wondered what Danny was feeling and whether he, too, wanted to make a contest out of this. He looked at Danny and the glance that came back told him all.

It was war.

'Push it, Jamie!'

'Come on, Danny!'

He noticed, with contempt, that both men were keeping their voices low so as not to attract Greg. Powell started to pace up and down in front of the bikes.

'Come on, Danny. He's weakening.'

Dad looked round at him in disgust.

▷ **2** *egg sb. on:* encourage sb. to do sth., esp. sth. they should not do **23** *lawsuit* ['lɔːsuːt]: Prozess, Klage **35** *ominous* ['ɒmɪnəs]: making you feel that sth. bad is going to happen in the future **39** *upstage sb.:* (here) show that you are better than sb. **49** *strain:* physical pressure · *tell:* (here) have a bad effect on sb./sth. **51** *yearn to do sth.:* want to do sth. very much **55** *ease up:* reduce the speed you are doing **65** *contempt:* Verachtung **66–67** *pace up and down:* walk up and down in a small area

'Weakening? Are you out of your mind? Danny's the one who's slowing down. Look, he's trying to save energy by not pedalling so hard.'

Danny shot him a venomous glance and put on speed. Powell scoffed.

'That's rubbish. Your boy's the one who's slowing down. Look at him. He's knackered.'

'He'll outlast your boy.'

'No way.'

'Fifty quid?'

'Done.'

Jamie stared at his father in disbelief. But Dad's eyes merely grew fiercer.

'Go on, Jamie, Give it your best.'

Powell laughed.

'If that's the best he's got, it won't take him very far.'

'Shut your mouth,' said Dad.

But Powell only laughed again.

Jamie dipped his head and tried to focus on the pedals. But his thoughts were confused now. They told him to stop because this was wrong. They told him not to stop because of what Dad would do to him if he lost.

But he was losing. He knew it.

He stole a glance to the side. Danny showed no signs of weakening and, if anything, seemed boosted by the element of competition. His mouth was open, gulping air, the sweat was vivid on his face; but he was clearly determined not to stop first.

If only Greg would come back. But there was still no sign of him.

The pain was almost unendurable now. He knew his face betrayed it. Like Danny, he was gulping in air but, unlike Danny, he was showing all his despair. Powell watched him for a few moments with an air of satisfaction, then threw a triumphant glance at Dad.

'Make it cash.'

Dad's answer came straight back, low and dangerous. 'Raise it.'

Powell stared at him. 'Are you out of your mind?'

'Raise it. Unless you're scared to.'

'For Christ's sake, just look at the kid. He's keeling over.'

Dad paused for a moment.

'A hundred,' he said, still not looking at Powell.

'You're crazy.'

'A hundred.'

'Look, I'm not doing this. I don't need your money that much.'

'So you are scared. I always knew you were.'

Jamie broke in, despite his exhaustion.

'Listen ... I ...'

Both men looked at him, and Danny, too, though he kept on pedalling. Jamie stared into his father's eyes and saw only a dark, unyielding obsession. And he could say no more.

Powell spoke again. 'I'm not raising the stakes. It's taking candy from a baby.'

Dad snorted. 'There's only one baby round here. And it's not Jamie.'

Powell's face darkened at once. 'All right. A hundred quid. And I'll see you damned.'

'Done. Excuse me if I don't shake hands.'

The two men turned back to the bikes.

But the contest was already over.

Jamie was falling. He remembered hearing them close the bet and turning to look at him. He remembered the terror of not being able to breathe, of feeling his legs numb and useless, his will spent, his balance gone. He remembered the floor, walls, ceiling slipping out of alignment, the handlebars moving closer. He remembered Greg running forward.

He remembered Dad's face.

Then nothing more.

▷ **4** *venomous* ['venəməs]: full of hatred **5** *scoff:* talk about sb./sth. in a way that shows you think they are not good **7** *knackered* (sl): extremely tired **8** *outlast sb./sth.:* continue doing sth. longer than sb./sth. **10** *quid* (BE, infml): pound (currency) **13** *fierce:* angry and aggressive in a way that is frightening **25** *boost sb.:* encourage sb. to do sth. better **34** *raise sth.:* increase the amount or level of sth. **37** *keel over:* fall over sidewards or forwards **48** *unyielding:* not easily influenced and unlikely to change **49** *the stakes:* money that is paid to the winners of a bet, etc. · *candy:* sweets **51** *snort:* make a sound through the nose to show that you think badly of sth. **54** *damned:* (here) totally defeated **60** *numb:* without feeling **61–62** *slip out of alignment* [ə'laɪnmənt]: (here) no longer remain where they should be

THIRTEEN

He was roused by the touch of fingers in his back. He opened his eyes to find himself lying on his stomach on the massage table in the treatment room. He didn't need to look round to see whose hands they were. But he twisted his head to see who else was here.

'Relax,' said Stephanie.

But he had seen all he needed. Dad wasn't here. That was all that mattered. He heard the door open, then Greg's voice.

'Finished, Steph?'

'Just about.' Stephanie bent down so that Jamie could see her without moving his head. 'You're so tensed up. Your body's like a spring. Even when you were asleep it was all knotted. It's better than it was when we started but you need a lot more of this. And a lot less of whatever's causing the problem.'

Greg drew up a chair and sat down where Jamie could see him.

'And we know what that is, don't we, Jamie?' He glanced at Stephanie. 'Haven't you got to pick up your kids? I thought they had a play rehearsal or something.'

'It's OK. Pete's picking them up.' She ruffled the top of Jamie's head. 'So I've got time to look after some of the bigger kids.'

Greg frowned.

'The really big kids have gone. But they're past helping anyway.'

Jamie stirred. 'You mean –?'

'I mean your dad's gone home. And the Powells.' He glanced up again. 'Go on, Steph. You've stayed on long enough. I'll get Jamie in the shower and take him home.'

She stood back from the table.

'OK. He's about as good as I'm going to get him today.' She leaned down again and smiled. 'Jamie, don't give us any more scares like that, OK?'

Jamie sighed. 'I'll try.' He paused, then: 'Thank you.'

'No problem. I'll see you around. Bye, Greg.'

'Bye, Steph. Thanks.'

Jamie breathed slowly, weary beyond anything he had ever known; and now desperately confused.

'What did my father say?'

Greg didn't try to hide his disgust.

'He said you're to walk home. Thought it would do you good, settle you down. But we both know that's not the reason, don't we?'

Jamie said nothing. Greg watched him for a moment.

'Listen, Jamie, it's none of my business and my mouth's got me into enough trouble over the years as it is, but I'm going to say this anyway. You're not enjoying training, you're not enjoying squash, you're not enjoying anything right now as far as I can see. I'm not going to say why because that's stating the obvious, but I'll tell you one thing. You're never going to be happy until you decide for yourself what you want in life and go after it in your own way.'

He paused for a moment.

'I'm afraid to say it'll probably mean getting into conflict while you assert yourself, and that'll hurt. Maybe a hell of a lot. But if you don't start taking steps to live your own life the way you want, you're going to end up getting hurt even more.'

Jamie rolled over onto his back and stared up at the ceiling, unsure what to say. Greg gave him a pat on the stomach.

'Right, end of lecture. Shower time. You should have had one earlier but we didn't have much choice over the order of events.'

'What happened?'

'You collapsed. We hoicked you in here and you came to, then fell asleep for the last half hour. The Powells packed up for the day and

▷ **1** *rouse sb.:* wake sb. **11** *spring:* (hier) Feder, Spirale · *knotted:* (here) hard and unrelaxed **18** *ruffle sth.:* disturb the surface of sth. so that it is no longer smooth **21** *be past sth.:* (here) be beyond sth. **28** *scare* (n): fright **30** *sigh* (v): take and let out a long deep breath **33** *weary:* very tired **44** *state the obvious:* say sth. unnecessary because it is clear to everyone **49** *assert oneself:* behave in a confident and determined way so that other people pay attention to your opinions **57** *hoick sb.* (infml): lift or pull sb. in a particular direction · *come to:* regain consciousness

left without finishing the programme. Your dad hung around just long enough for Steph to look you over and tell him you weren't going to die, then he cleared off. I saw money changing hands between him and Bob. I didn't ask any questions and I don't want any answers. Right, let's get you on your feet.'

'I'm OK. It's all right.' Jamie stood up, awkwardly.

'You look a bit dizzy.'

'It's OK. I can manage.'

Greg walked with him to the changing room and switched on the shower for him. Jamie took off his clothes and climbed under. The sluicing water felt good but he was still desperately tired.

Greg leaned against the wall outside the shower, his body blurred through the opaque glass of the door.

'I worry about you, Jamie. Haven't heard you laugh for a long time. What do you do when you're not training or playing squash?'

'Nothing much.'

'You got a girlfriend?'

'No.'

'But you've got mates?'

'I've got one. My father doesn't approve of him.'

He saw Greg shift his position outside.

'Jamie, like I say, you're going to have to sort out what you really want. If it's to be a squash champion, that's fine. Squash is a great game. But don't deceive yourself. If you're not enjoying it any more, then it's time to stop or ease up. And try and find space in your life for something other than squash, like meeting more people, for example, preferably people who aren't interested in squash.'

'Spider's like that.'

'Who?'

'My friend.'

'Is that his name?

'It's a nickname. Everyone calls him Spider. He thinks squash is a stupid game. He's more interested in deciding which girl to go out with on a Friday night.'

'Well, he sounds the kind of boy you want to see more of. When you've done showering and got dressed, come to my office and I'll run you home.'

But Jamie no longer knew where home was.

He stood outside his house, shivering in the chilly air, and stared at it through the darkness. All the curtains were drawn but the lights were on in the sitting room and his parents' bedroom. He waited until Greg's car had gone, then walked up to the front door, put the key in the lock and turned it.

Inside the hall he paused for a moment and listened, the door still open behind him. From the sitting room came the noise of the television, but he also heard sounds upstairs, the heavy footsteps of his father moving about the bedroom. He closed the door quietly and hurried through to the sitting room.

Mum was sitting on the sofa when he entered but she stood up at once.

'Darling, what's happened?'

He looked at her, wondering what to say. Dad would have given her his version of things already, and that would no doubt be the one that would count for her. But her eyes held no accusation. And he could tell that the tension she had shown at breakfast was still there. If anything, it was worse.

He tried to keep his mind on what he had to do.

'I had a problem at the gym. There's something I've got to talk to Dad about.'

'He said you weren't feeling well.'

'More than that.'

She stared at him. 'What do you mean?'

'Didn't he tell you?'

He studied her face and saw a conflict of emotions. It was some moments before she answered.

'He … told me you were on the exercise bike and … Danny was there and you … you didn't feel very well so you stopped. And he agreed with you that it would be best for you to walk home because you needed some fresh air. And Mr Mason was looking after you.'

Jamie looked away, trying to control the anger that now flooded through him. Somehow he kept his voice calm.

'Do you want to know what really happened? I'll tell you.'

But at that moment Dad entered the room.

▷ **3** *clear off* (infml): go away **7** *dizzy:* feeling as if everything is spinning around you **11** *sluice* [sluːs]: flow in large quantities **24** *deceive sb.:* make sb. believe sth. that is not true **36–37** *run sb. somewhere:* drive sb. somewhere

Jamie stiffened and tried to marshal his thoughts into words. But Dad spoke first.

'Are you feeling better?'

The question took him by surprise. He had expected some kind of reprimand. He sensed Mum close by, rigidly still. He looked at Dad.

'I'm … OK. Now.'

'Good.'

'But I'm tired. I'm really tired. And I …' He took a deep breath, his thoughts racing. He had to say this now, before his will wavered. 'I've decided –'

'You'd better get some food inside you. Your mum's got something for you in the oven, I think.' Dad glanced at Mum, clearly expecting her to go and attend to that. But she took a step towards him.

'What happened at the gym?'

Dad frowned. 'I told you what happened.'

'Something else happened. Something you haven't told me.'

Jamie stared at her. She never questioned Dad like this. Dad still frowned.

'I've told you everything that happened,' he said. 'And what needs to happen now is for Jamie to get some food inside him.'

Mum hesitated, then looked round at Jamie.

'There is some food. I'll … I'll put it out for you on the kitchen table. It'll be a few minutes because I want to do some peas. But I …' She glanced at Dad. 'I … I still want to know –'

Dad cut her off. 'There's nothing more to tell. You're worrying about nothing.'

She stared at him, her face clouded with confusion, then she bit her lip and left the room.

Jamie clenched his fists. Her resistance had ended so quickly. But now his had to start.

'I've … I've come to a decision.'

Dad said nothing. Jamie dropped his eyes.

'I've come to a decision. I … I want to stop.'

'Stop what?'

Jamie forced himself to look up.

'I want to stop squash.'

'I presume that's a joke.'

'Its not a joke.'

'Then I'll overlook it because you're tired.'

‘I am tired but it’s not … because I’m tired. I’ve thought about this and I’ve … I’ve decided. I want to stop.’

Dad’s face darkened.

‘Are you out of your mind? You’ve spent your life training to be a champion. You’ve spent hours in the gym, hours on the running track, hours on court and so have I. I’ve put all my effort and not a little expense into turning you into a future winner, and all you can say, after an evening at the gym that didn’t go too well and which – incidentally – cost me a hundred quid, is that you’re giving up. Well, you can wipe that idea out of your mind right now. I’m not listening to any of it.’

‘I –’

‘I’m not listening to any of it, do you understand?’ Dad’s voice rose. ‘What hurts me most is your ingratitude. I’ve given up practically all my waking hours to your success. You’d be nowhere without the time and money I’ve invested in you. You were born with talent and you’ve got everything going for you. And you want to throw it all away.’

Jamie looked down again. This wasn’t how he’d intended it. But then, he’d known his father would argue with him. He swallowed hard.

‘I just … I just –’

‘I’m disappointed in you, Jamie. I’m so disappointed. I came back tonight determined to give you a second chance after you made a fool of me in front of Bob Powell. I’m prepared to let that go and –’

‘I collapsed. Are you saying that was my fault?’

‘Of course it was your fault. Who else’s fault was it? If you’d been putting the right amount of effort into your training, you’d have been able to stick it out on the exercise bike. Danny managed it. So why couldn’t you?’

▷ **2** *marshal sth.:* gather sth. together and organise it/them **6** *reprimand* ['reprɪmɑːnd] (n): act of telling sb. that you do not approve of them and their actions · *rigid* ['rɪdʒɪd] stiff **10** *waver* ['weɪvə]: become weak **28** *clouded with sth.:* showing sth. (esp. an unpleasant emotion) **30** *clench your fists:* die Fäuste ballen **40** *overlook sth.:* ignore sth. which you consider wrong or bad **44** *be out of your mind* (infml): be crazy **49** *incidentally:* by the way **53** *ingratitude:* state of not feeling or showing that you are thankful for sth. **66** *be sb.'s fault:* be the responsibility of sb. that sth. went wrong **69** *stick sth. out* (infml): continue doing sth. to the end

Jamie felt himself tremble. It was no good. He would never get through to his father.

'Look, I can't take any more of this. I'm going.'

He took a step towards the door. But Dad caught him by the arm.

'I haven't finished speaking to you, yet.'

Jamie stared at him for a moment, then tried again to walk on. Dad gripped his arm more tightly.

'I said I haven't finished speaking.'

Jamie looked once more into the dark, unyielding eyes, and they scared him.

'I want to go,' he said, and tried to pull his arm away. But Dad thrust him back against the wall and pinned him there.

'I've worked all my life for what I've got. I've struggled in ways you'll never know. And all I've ever wanted was for you to have the chances I never had. And now I've given you those chances, you –'

Jamie saw what was coming and ducked. Too late. Dad's hand struck him hard in the side of the face. He struggled to free himself but the hand swung in again, and again, and again, Dad spitting out words with each blow.

'Ungrateful ... little ... shit ... bloody ... little ... shit.'

Jamie fell back, breaking from Dad's grasp. His foot caught the poker standing by the fire and sent it clattering over the hearthstones. He grabbed the edge of the mantelpiece and clung to it, trying to keep his balance. Dad seized him by the scruff of the neck and pulled him up until their faces were inches apart.

'If you ever do this to me again, I'll really teach you what discipline means.'

In the darkness, he made his way past his parents' room and down to the hall. There he stopped and listened.

The house was still. He crept through to the kitchen, loaded his rucksack, and checked his watch.

Midnight.

He thought of Mum again and in his mind saw her face as she stood in the doorway after Dad had left him, and watched in silence, before retreating to the bedroom.

He tiptoed to the back door, opened it as quietly as he could and closed it after him. Then he shouldered the rucksack, slipped out of the back gate and hurried away towards the town.

FOURTEEN

There was no sign of the girl in the alleyway by the health food shop but he wasn't surprised. This was the last place he'd have wanted to go to alone, now that he thought about it, and he felt sure that even if she had considered coming to meet him, she would probably have taken one look at the dark entrance and changed her mind. He should have thought of a better meeting-place.

He looked around him uneasily. There had been several muggings in this part of town and all kinds of violent episodes after dark. The pubs had emptied some time ago but there was no knowing what kind of people might be lurking round here.

A car beam cut through the darkness, catching the side of the shops as it fanned down towards him. He stepped back inside the entrance to the alley and hid himself in the shadows. A few moments later, a police car swept past. And silence fell.

Then he heard a voice.

'You're late.'

He whirled round, startled, but saw nothing.

'Here.'

The voice came from further down the alley. He walked to where the passageway twisted round at the end and saw the girl slumped on the ground, her back against the wall, her holdall beside her.

▷ **9** *unyielding:* not easily influenced **12** *thrust sb.:* push sb. quickly and violently · *pin sb.:* make sb. unable to move **22** *poker:* metal stick for moving coal in a fire **22** *hearthstone* ['hɑːθstəʊn]: stones that make up the bottom of a fireplace **23** *mantelpiece:* shelf above a fireplace **45** *mugging* (n): violent attack on a person in order to steal money **48** *lurk:* wait somewhere secretly because you are going to do sth. bad or illegal

'Have you got any food?' she said bluntly.

He looked at her for a moment, then started to undo the rucksack. She spoke again, slightly less abruptly.

'Sorry. Being hungry takes away your manners.'

'It's OK.'

He handed her one of the sandwiches he'd made up in the kitchen. She took it without a word and started wolfing it down with the same intensity as the last time he had seen her eat. He let her finish the sandwich, then spoke again.

'Are you cold?'

'What do you think?'

'Only ...' He paused. 'I've thought of a way of getting you warm tonight.'

She looked at him suspiciously.

'It's all right,' he said. 'You can trust me. I promise.'

She held his gaze for a few more seconds, then sniffed and looked away.

'Sorry. I know you're trying to help.'

'I didn't think you'd be here.'

'Neither did I.'

'So what made you –?' He broke off, sensing a slight embarrassment in her. 'Come on,' he said. 'I can find a warmer place than this.'

He stood up and waited to see if she would move, too. She started to struggle to her feet. He hesitated, having momentarily forgotten she was pregnant, then reached out a hand. She took it at once and he pulled.

Her hand felt cold but she was soon on her feet and let go of his hand at once. He picked up his rucksack.

'Let's go.'

'Wait,' she said.

He turned. 'What's up?'

'Those men you told me about. Have you seen them tonight?'

'No.'

'Only ... I don't want to bump into them.'

'Neither do I. So that's not a problem.'

'You don't understand. This ...' She looked at him hard. 'This ... isn't a game. It could be dangerous. I told you before. You shouldn't get involved in my life. There's nothing I can give you except trouble.'

He looked down.

'I don't want anything from you. You don't owe me anything. You've got your troubles and you don't need to tell me about them if you don't want to. Anyway, I've … I've got troubles of my own. I won't burden you with them, but I …' He took a deep breath. 'I've left home. I'm going to have people looking for me from tomorrow morning. Police, probably, and my parents, and maybe other people. People who know me. But …'

He looked up again and saw her eyes fixed on his. He went on.

'I won't be going home again. I need to get away, somewhere, anywhere, away from Ashingford. There'll be too many people who recognize me. I don't know what I'm going to do. I haven't got any money. I haven't got any food apart from what I've stuffed in my rucksack, and that was meant for you anyway. I haven't got any plan of what I'm going to do. I …' He looked down again. 'I'm a mess. A complete bloody mess.'

She said nothing and he didn't look up. He felt sure, now that he'd told her all this, that she would walk on and leave him. With all that she had on her mind, the last thing she would want now was a lame duck on her hands. But she spoke to him.

'So we're both shadows.'

He looked up. 'What?'

'Shadows. I thought it was just me. But you're the same, aren't you? Maybe we need each other for a little while.'

'But why shadows?

She looked hard at him.

'When you live in the shadows long enough, you become one.'

They walked down the main street, keeping close to the buildings.

'Don't walk so fast,' she said. 'I can't keep up. And if you see those men, tell me. If necessary, we split, right? And meet again later.'

'Where?'

'Back in the alleyway. But with any luck, it won't happen.'

'I haven't seen them around tonight.'

▷ **1** *blunt:* direct without politeness **4** *manners:* polite behaviour **35** *bump into sb.*: meet sb. accidentally **42** *troubles:* problems **44** *burden sb.with sth.:* jdn. mit etwas belasten **54** *be a mess* (infml): feel that nothing is right in your life **58–59** *a lame duck:* a person that is not very successful and needs help **69** *split:* go separate ways

'I have. One's in a car. The other's walking the streets. They keep in touch by mobile phone.'

Jamie frowned. 'These men ... I mean ... who –?'

'I don't want to talk about them,' she said. 'Just tell me if you see them, OK?'

She fell silent and he could tell from the set of her face that she didn't want him to probe further.

'Which way to this place of yours?' she said.

'I'll show you.'

He led her past the clock tower and away from the town centre, a feeling of unreality creeping over him as he walked through the streets with this strange vagrant girl.

He stopped suddenly.

'What's up?' she said, stopping, too.

'I don't even know your name.'

She looked at him. 'Shadows don't have names.'

They walked on for a few minutes in silence. Then she spoke.

'Listen, we need to have an understanding. You don't tell me anything you don't want and I don't tell you anything I don't want, OK?'

'OK.'

'You've got your life and I've got mine. We don't need to know anything else. We're just two people sticking together for a little while and then we'll go our separate ways.'

He dug his chin into the top of his coat.

'OK.'

'How much further?'

'Just up this lane.'

'But there's only a school up there.'

'I know.'

Again he saw suspicion on her face. But he could understand that. The school lane was a lonely place at night.

'It's OK,' he said. He thought for a moment. 'I'm not going to do you any harm.'

She shrugged. 'Well, let's get a move on. I'm freezing.'

He led her down the lane, gazing ahead at the sombre outlines of the buildings and the trees around the playing field. A few minutes later they reached the school gate.

'Now what?' she said.

'Bit further,' he said and walked on past the gate. She followed, lagging behind now and clearly very tired. Finally he reached the gap in the fence and stopped. She caught up with him and examined the opening.

'Through this?'

'Yes.'

'You first.'

He bent down and squeezed through, wondering as he did so whether she would follow. Somehow he felt their alliance hung on the most slender of threads, one which could break at any moment. But when he straightened up on the other side, she was still there, watching him.

'Where are we going after this?' she said.

'I'll show you when you get through.' He saw her hesitate and added: 'I promise you it's very warm.'

She seemed to come to a decision, bent down and started to squeeze herself through. For her it was more of a struggle. The fence opening, loosened and worked by countless hands on countless occasions, was only prepared to give so much. She reached out a hand.

'Help me.'

He took it and pulled, and a moment later they were standing together on the soggy playing field. She let go his hand.

'Where to now?'

'Not far.'

He led the way across the playing field, keeping his eyes alert for movements around them. But all seemed still. He heard her shiver behind him and glanced over his shoulder.

'How have you been keeping warm at nights? When you weren't in my shed, I mean.'

She said nothing for a while and he thought back to what she had said about not talking about themselves if they didn't want to. But she answered him.

▷ **7** *probe* (v): ask questions to find out secret or hidden information **25** *dig – dug – dug sth. into sth. else:* etwas in etwas (ver)graben **31** *suspicion:* Misstrauen **36** *sombre* ['sɒmbə]: dark **41** *lag behind:* move more slowly than other people **42** *catch up with sb.:* join sb. who was going faster **47** *squeeze through:* manage to get through a small opening **48** *alliance* [ə'laɪəns]: agreement to stay together **49** *slender:* very thin · *thread:* Faden **58** *give:* nachgeben **61** *soggy:* wet and soft

'Depends on where I was. I spent one night standing in a public loo, pressing the hand-drier to keep warm.' She paused. 'You need to think hard before you take on this kind of life.'

He frowned and walked on across the field. At last they were there. He stopped and turned to her. 'This is it.'

She stared up at the building before them. 'What's this place?'

'The squash court. Come on.'

He started to make his way round to the door. But she caught his arm.

'What is it?' he said.

'Ssh!'

She tightened her grip and he stood still, wondering what was wrong. Then he heard it, too. The sound of a car, far down the lane. He turned and saw headlights approaching.

She tugged at his arm. 'Quick! Get behind the building.'

They hurried round the side of the squash court and stopped by the door. Jamie threw the rucksack to the ground and fumbled with the catch.

'What are you doing?' she said.

'Looking for the key.'

'The what?'

'The key. To the squash court.'

The loom of the lights was growing brighter as the car drew nearer. In a moment it would be level with them and they would be visible through the fence. He found the key, turned it in the lock and pulled open the door.

'Get in!'

She didn't hesitate but hurried inside. He jumped after her, closed the door and locked it from the inside, then took out the key. They stared at each other in the darkness, both breathing hard.

The sound of the engine grew louder, then, as the car drew level with the building, the tone changed to a tick-over. He saw the alarm in her face.

'They're stopping,' she whispered.

He tried to think of something to say to reassure her.

'They might not have seen us. And it might –'

'Keep your voice low,' she hissed.

He took a deep breath and went on, whispering as she had done.

'It might not be those men. It might just be a police patrol. Or a couple of lovers or something.'

She leaned back against the wall and stared ahead of her.

'It's them. I recognized the car.'

He, too, leaned against the wall, and they both listened. The engine fell silent, then one of the car doors opened and shut, and, a moment later, the other door. He clenched his fists. They must have been spotted. And here they were, trapped in this cage. He glanced at the girl. And stiffened.

Never in his life had he seen a face like that. It was racked with fear. He knew then that whatever part these men had played so far in this girl's life, it was a terrible one.

He reached out a hand.

She didn't see it, didn't look his way when she felt it; but she held it, tight, so tight that he was on the point of asking her to relax her grip – when he heard a new sound.

Footsteps.

They must have climbed over the fence or slipped through the hole.

The girl's hand tightened still further. He tried desperately to think. The door was locked – that was one thing – and it was the only way in. They would have to break it down to get at them. That would make a fair bit of noise, though it was doubtful anyone would hear them. There was no one around the school buildings at this time of night.

Or perhaps they would pick the lock.

The door-knob twisted suddenly.

He felt his hand squeezed again, so sharply that he nearly yelped.

The door did not open. The knob twisted back and was still. He looked at the girl in the darkness and tried to give her a reassuring glance. But all he saw in her face was terror.

The door-knob twisted once more, then flicked back to its normal position.

▷ **12** *tighten your grip:* hold on to sb. in a firmer way **17** *fumble with sth.:* have difficulty with sth. **18** *catch* (n): device used to lock a door **23** *loom of the lights:* Lichtkegel **31** *draw level with sb./sth.:* come up beside sb./sth. **32** *tick-over:* Leerlauf **37** *hiss* (v): speak in an angry whisper **48** *racked with sth.:* full of sth. (esp. strong unpleasant emotions) **63** *pick a lock:* open a door using a piece of wire, etc. **64** *door-knob:* round door handle · *twist* (v): turn

A moment later, he heard feet tramping away. He breathed out and opened his mouth to whisper. She squeezed his hand at once and he saw her eyes fixed on him with fierce intensity. Her finger was at her lips. He nodded to reassure her, and said nothing.

She still watched him but seemed relieved now that she knew he wasn't going to speak. She let go his hand, and it seemed to him a sign that she was regaining control of herself. He thought of the tension he had felt in that hand, and looked away, feeling strangely vulnerable himself now that it was gone.

He listened, yearning for the sound of car doors and the engine revving up again. But those sounds did not come. Somewhere outside, the men were still roaming.

He heard a sharp click in the direction of the main buildings. It sounded as though they were trying the door to one of the prefab classrooms. If so, there might yet be hope. The men might not have seen them enter the squash court after all.

Silence fell once again, then there was another click, further to the left. That sounded like the PE storeroom. He strained his ears and listened for more sounds. They tried another door, then another, then footsteps approached again. He tensed, certain they would try the squash court door once more.

But they went straight past, back towards the fence. He looked at the girl. She was staring ahead, her face taut as she listened for the sounds they both longed to hear.

At last they came. One car door opened and closed, then the other. The engine started and revved up, then they heard the car turn in the lane and motor off towards the town.

The girl gave a sigh. 'That was close.'

He stared at her.

'I can't work out what made them come here. I didn't see them following us. And I thought they'd be hanging around the shed tonight. But they must have seen us somehow. Why would they go to all the trouble of coming out here if there wasn't good reason?'

She glanced at him.

'There was good reason. I dossed at the school one night, before I found your shed.'

'What, not in here?'

She shook her head.

'Wish I could have done. You're right. It's warm. No, I used the girls' loo by the PE hut. There was no problem getting in there. It was freezing but it seemed a safer place than the streets. I didn't think they'd look for me inside a school.'

'But how did you get in?'

'You're not the only one who knows about the hole in the fence.'

'But have they actually seen you here?'

She thought for a moment.

'Don't think so. But lots of other people saw me in the lane and if the men have been asking questions in town, it's possible someone might have said they've seen me here.' She shrugged. 'Well, hopefully it'll all be over soon. Have you got any more food?'

'Sure.'

'And is there a changing room in here somewhere? I've got to sit down. I don't feel too good.'

He looked at her.

'What ... you mean ...?'

'Yeah. The baby.'

'Is it due soon?'

'Never mind that. I want to sit down.'

He nodded to the right.

'There's a girls' changing room down that end. It's got a loo and I think there's a radiator in there. There's one in the boys' changing room anyway.' He nodded to the left. 'Up there.'

'Which is more comfortable?'

'Don't know. I never go in the girls' changing room. The boys' is a bit primitive.'

She walked down to the girls' changing room and glanced round the door, but didn't switch on the light. A moment later she came back.

'Let's try your changing room.'

He led the way past the open door to the squash court, a curious symbol now of a life that seemed to belong to someone else, and entered the boys' changing room.

She followed and sat straight down on the bench nearest the radiator. He joined her, rummaged in the rucksack for the

▷ **11** *rev up:* (of an engine) start up quickly and noisily **12** *roam:* walk around without definite aim or direction **14** *prefab:* Fertigbau- **18** *PE storeroom:* room used to keep equipment for Physical Education (i.e. sports lessons) **23** *taut* [tɔːt]: showing that you are anxious and tense **57** *be due:* be time to be born

sandwiches and handed her one. She took it and leaned back against the wall.

'Thanks.'

He watched her for a moment as she ate with that same desperate urgency, then leaned back, too, fighting his own hunger.

'Aren't you going to eat?' she said.

'No. I had a big meal before I came out. The sandwiches are all for you.'

She did not seem to detect the lie and went on eating. After a while she closed her eyes and dozed.

But Jamie did not even try to doze. He knew his thoughts would not let him. Instead, as she slept, he stared out at the dark cell of the room and wondered about the future.

FIFTEEN

She only slept for about an hour, and her sleep was fitful and jerky. Then she woke and asked for another sandwich. He handed her one and leaned back again, watching her.

She finished the sandwich in silence, then suddenly looked round at him.

'Those men, they're ...' She paused. 'Listen, I don't want any questions about things I don't want to tell you, OK?'

'We've already agreed that.'

'So don't push me.'

'I'm not going to.'

She paused again, as though waiting for him to say more. But he remained silent. She went on.

'I'm in serious trouble. You must have worked that out already. I'm not from round here – you've maybe worked that out, too – but I had to come to try and sort something out.'

She breathed hard.

'Those two men ... I owe them money. A lot of money. Much more money than I can lay my hands on. And they want it badly. Not just that, they want revenge. I haven't got a bean on me and I'm terrified of what they'll do to me if they catch me. And I'm frightened for the baby.'

Something in her manner seemed to soften as she uttered the last word. She'd thrown out the other words all at once, as though to rid

▷ **11** *doze:* sleep lightly for a short time **14** *fitful:* not continuous or regular · *jerky:* making sudden starts and stops **32** *not have a bean* (infml): have no money **35** *rid sb. of sth.:* remove sth. that is a problem from sb.

herself of them as quickly as possible. But the mention of the baby changed her completely.

He sat up. 'How much money do you owe them?'

'You don't want to know. But it's a lot. Several thousand.'

'How many thousand?'

She looked down and spoke, in such a low voice that he barely caught the answer. But he heard; and it made him whistle.

'How the hell did you get that much in debt?'

There was a long silence, and he realized he had just broken the rule of not asking questions. Sure enough, she wasn't prepared to tell him.

'I don't want to talk about it. But they're dangerous, OK? You're best off not associating with me.'

He hesitated.

'This money, did you, I mean ...?'

'Did I steal it?' She almost snarled at him. 'No, I didn't. I'm not a criminal. I might have taken money from your house but this money was legitimate so if you bloody well think –'

'I don't, I don't.' He held out a hand. 'I don't think anything. Please don't get angry. I'm not accusing you of anything.'

She had sat bolt upright but quickly slumped back on the bench again. He cursed himself silently for overstepping the mark, especially when there was no need. He had already worked out who the enemy was. He looked at her and spoke as gently as he could.

'Those men, would they leave you alone if you paid them the money?'

'What difference does it make? I can't pay them anyway. Not now.'

'What do you mean, not now?'

She glanced across at him and again he sensed her reluctance to talk.

'Listen,' he said. 'I know there are things you don't want to tell me. That's fine. There are things I don't want to tell you. But let me ask you things and if I ask you something you don't want to talk about, don't bite my head off. Just say you don't want to talk about it, and that's no problem.'

She seemed to relax slightly; and after a moment's thought, she answered him.

'I came here to try and get the money to pay them off. I know someone who I thought ... might give me the money and I could somehow send it to them, without having to meet them. But ... well, I can't get the money from him.'

He studied her face. The darkness had softened it and it seemed strangely childlike. It occurred to him with a slight shock that they had never actually seen each other in the daylight. Perhaps she was right. They were shadows after all.

'But just for argument's sake,' he said, 'if you did pay them off, would they leave you alone then?'

She pulled her coat round her shoulders.

'Maybe, maybe not. They're not the men to forgive. They'd probably take the money, then sort me.'

He looked at her. 'You mean ...?'

'I mean they'd kill me. At the very least, they'd make sure I never win any beauty contests.'

She looked down suddenly.

'Why the hell are you getting involved? It's nothing to do with you, all this. You don't owe me anything. Nobody owes me anything.' She shook her head. 'You're nice and I know you mean well but you should be thinking about your own problems and leave me to sort out mine. I told you, I can't give you anything back.'

'I don't want anything back. Listen –' He looked down again. 'My life's in a mess, too, and maybe, I don't know, maybe I just ... need a friend for a little while, just like you need a friend, for a little while. That's all. No strings attached. Just a couple of shadows, like you said, sticking together, until we can go our separate ways.'

She didn't speak and he kept his eyes riveted to the floor, but he sensed her watching him in the darkness. He spoke again, his voice small and tense.

'I'm really scared. Not scared like you were just now when the men were outside. I know my problem's nothing compared with yours. But I'm still scared. I don't know what's happened to my life. I don't know where I'm going or what I'm doing. I don't know anything about tomorrow.'

▷ **16** *snarl:* speak in an angry or bad-tempered way **21** *bolt upright:* with your back straight **22** *overstep the mark:* behave in a way that is not thought to be acceptable **29** *reluctance:* unwillingness to do sth. **46** *for argument's sake:* rein theoretisch **50** *sort sb. (out):* (infml): (here) deal with sb. who is causing trouble **63** *no strings attached:* no special conditions or restrictions **65** *riveted* ['rɪvɪtɪd]: fixed

To his surprise, he felt her hand touch his. He took it and held it, glad for it, until embarrassment seemed to master them both, and their hands slid apart once more.

He looked round at her. 'You said earlier that all this would hopefully be over soon. What did you mean?'

'I'm leaving Ashingford tomorrow. I told you, I came down to try and borrow the money to pay them off but ... well, anyway, I couldn't do it. So I'll just have to go to ground and keep looking over my shoulder.'

She yawned.

'I've got an address in Cumbria, friends of a friend. They'll hide me, help with the baby, keep me out of the way for a bit until I can move on. If I can slip away from here without being spotted.'

'Will these people pay the men off?'

'No. It's just a sanctuary, for me and the baby, when it comes. I was going to go straight there but I decided to come here first and try to get the money.'

She yawned again.

'Better get a bit more rest. I'll have to set off before daylight. It's too dangerous for me to move around when it's light. I should be heading for the motorway now but I'm too tired. I'll just have to get through another day lying low and start hitching in the evening.'

She looked at him suddenly. 'We'll have to split after we leave this building.'

Jamie leaned closer.

'Listen, I won't get in your way. I won't do anything that causes you problems but ... can I come with you? To Cumbria, I mean. Just to make sure you get to your sanctuary. I won't stay, not long. But I want to help you and, like I said, I ... I need a friend myself. Just for a bit.'

She seemed to ponder his words for a long time. Then she shrugged.

'OK.'

They didn't sleep. They tried to doze, lying on the benches, then sitting up, backs against the wall, and finally, without a word between them, moved to the corner of the room, where two benches joined, and stretched out, lying in opposite directions, his head in the crook of her shoulder, hers in the crook of his.

After about an hour, she sat up. 'We should be going. I can't sleep anyway.'

He sat up, too. 'OK. When do you want to start hitching tonight?'

'When it looks safe. We've got to get across Ashingford to the roundabout on the ring road where the motorway starts. That'll take a while. I can't walk very fast.'

He thought for a moment about the idea that had been growing in his mind.

'Listen,' he said. 'There's something I've got to do. Something I've got to sort out. Can we split when we get out of here and meet up this evening?'

'You walking out on me already?'

'No, it's not that.'

'I'm not bothered if you do.'

'No, OK, but ... I mean ... I'm not. I've just got some things to sort out, too. So what time do you want to meet at the roundabout?'

'I won't wait for you. If you're not there, tough.'

'Fair enough. But what time?'

She thought for a moment. 'Call it six o'clock tomorrow evening.'

'This evening. Not tomorrow evening.'

She shrugged. 'Whatever. But I told you, I'm not waiting for you.'

'I'll be there.'

She looked at him for a moment. 'OK. But don't meet me at the roundabout itself. It's too exposed. Anyone can see you.'

'So where shall we meet?'

'Get to the roundabout, OK?'

'Right.'

'Take the slip-road that goes up towards the motorway, then look up to your right. There are some slabs of concrete supporting the motorway, where the flyover meets the verge. If you climb up inside them, they make a kind of room underneath the carriageway. It's not

▷ **2** *master sth.:* control sth. **8** *go to ground* (infml): hide **11** *Cumbria:* mountainous county in NW England **15** *sanctuary:* safe place in which you are protected from your enemies **22** *hitch:* get a free ride in sb.'s car **43** *roundabout:* Kreisverkehr · *ring road:* Umgehungsstraße **50** *walk out on sb.:* leave sb. **55** *tough* [tʌf]: that's unfortunate for you **66** *slip-road:* road used for driving onto or off a motorway **67** *slab:* thick, flat piece · *concrete* ['kɒŋkriːt]: Beton **68** *flyover*: bridge that carries one road over another one · *verge:* area of grass at the side of a road **69** *carriageway:* one of the two sides of a motorway

a very good doss but once you're in there, you can't be seen from the road.'

She grimaced suddenly and clutched her stomach.

He reached out and held her by the arm.

'Is it –?'

'Of course it is.' She reached out with her other hand and held on to one of the locker handles. 'God, if this baby comes early ... I don't think I can handle that on top of everything else. It's not due for another two weeks. I'd been ... counting on having it up north where these people can help me.'

'Are you sure you're fit to move?'

She looked at him.

'What choice have I got?' She stiffened and lurched towards the door. 'Come on. Let's get out of here.'

She was breathing hard and didn't look well enough to move but he said nothing and followed her to the door of the building. They both listened for sounds outside.

All was quiet.

'Have you got a watch?' she said.

'Yeah.' He looked down at it. 'Half-past four.'

'It's about the right time to move, while there's still darkness. I just wish it wasn't so cold.'

He unlocked the door, opened it and stepped out. The coldness of the night air struck him at once. She joined him outside the building and shivered.

'Wish we could have stayed a bit longer,' he said, locking the door again.

Suddenly she gripped his arm.

'What is it?' he said.

'Be quiet.'

He looked around them yet he could see nothing threatening, only the outlines of the school buildings and further down, across the field, the outer fence which ran alongside the lane. She leaned closer, still gripping his arm.

'Is there another way out of this school?'

He nodded towards the main buildings.

'If you go round the side of the main block and past the library building, you come to the gym. On the other side of that there's another fence. But you'd have to climb over. There's no hole. We're better off going the way we came in.'

He winced suddenly as she squeezed his arm tight.

And then he understood.

From the other side of the playing field two figures were racing towards the squash court.

▷ **7** *locker:* small cupboard in which to leave clothes etc. after changing for sport **13** *lurch* (v): make a sudden unsteady movement forward **41** *wince:* suddenly make an expression with your face that shows that you are feeling pain

SIXTEEN

'Quick!' said Jamie. 'Towards the main buildings.'

He dropped the rucksack and started to run. The girl struggled with him, clutching her bag, her face screwed up with fear. But she could not go fast and he knew they wouldn't get far like this.

He glanced back at the two men. They must have worked out that he and the girl were still somewhere on the school grounds and had hung around waiting. They were still a few hundred yards away but there was no chance of outrunning them. He could get away easily but the girl wouldn't. They would have to hide. And there was only one place he could think of.

'Hurry!' he said. 'Round the side of the main building.'

They stumbled round the corner and he ran ahead to the big dustbins at the back of the school kitchen. The first one was full, the second almost empty. The girl caught him up, breathlessly.

'Get in!' he said.

She didn't argue and tried to lift herself over the side of the bin.

'I can't do it,' she said. 'It's too high.'

He heard the panic in her voice.

'Easy, easy,' he said. He pulled over a small wooden crate. 'Stand on that.'

It broke under her weight the moment she stepped on it.

He looked frantically towards the corner of the building. The men would be here any moment. Beside him the girl was trembling uncontrollably. Maybe they should run, look for somewhere else to hide.

But he knew of nowhere. And the seconds were running out. It had to be the bin.

'Come on. I'll give you a leg-up.'

He locked his fingers together and made a support. She placed her foot in the cradle of his hands and somehow climbed in. He handed her the holdall and the broken crate, then made to close the lid.

She looked out at him, her face small and petrified.

'Don't leave me! Please don't leave me!'

He knew he dare not linger. If the men saw him by the bins, all would be lost. But he had to comfort her somehow.

'Just stay as quiet as you can with the lid down. I'll try and lead the men away from here somehow. We'll meet where we said, at the motorway.'

'But –'

'There's no time. I've got to go.'

He closed the lid before she could answer. Then, on an impulse, opened it again.

'I won't desert you. I promise.'

He closed the lid again and raced down towards the science huts. Somehow he had to make them see him and think she was with him. He reached the corner of the Physics lab, stopped and looked back.

The men appeared round the side of the main building and stopped, looking around them. They had not spotted him yet. The taller one walked forward to the bin in which the girl was hiding and put his hand on the lid.

Jamie stepped into view, as though he had just come from behind the Physics lab and shouted as if to someone behind it. 'Go on! Go on!'

He didn't know if they were taken in by this but at least they had left the bins.

He ran down the side of the lab and cut through the other prefab huts in the science area. Footsteps sounded hard on his heels.

He called out again, as if to the girl. 'Go that way! Through the hole in the fence by the gym!'

▷ **13** *dustbin:* large container used for putting rubbish in **19** *crate:* wooden box **22** *frantic:* unable to control your emotions because you are extremely frightened or worried **28** *give sb. a leg-up* (infml): help sb. climb on or over sth. **32** *petrified* ['petrɪfaɪd]: extremely frightened **34** *linger* ['lɪŋgə]: stay for longer than is necessary **64** *take sb. in:* make sb. believe sth. that is not true

He listened again for their footsteps but suddenly there were none. He stopped, anxious not to give his position away, and strained to hear them.

There was not a sound but he did not doubt they were moving close by. He stared round at the huts, searching for movement.

Somehow he had to get away. He crept to the edge of the Chemistry lab. There was no sign of the men but that made him warier still. Down to his left were the tennis courts and gym. There was no hole in the fence there but it was just possible the men had heard him and gone to check it out. He looked about him, saw nothing, and started to run towards the Home Economics huts.

The next moment, a hand seized him by the shoulder.

The taller man had him by the scruff of the neck. He felt himself pushed back against the side of the building. Then the shorter man appeared.

Jamie looked from one to the other. There was no chance of escape but he might still do some good.

'Run for it!' he shouted in the direction of the gym. 'Run for it!'

He hoped the girl would not hear him from inside the bin and think he meant her to climb out. But there was no time to think of that now. The taller man pulled out a knife, then glanced round at his companion.

'You go after the girl. She won't get far the way she's moving. I'll just settle up with young Jamie.'

'Which way?' said the other man.

'The way our friend just told us. Go on, quick. Before she finds a place to hide. I'll be along in a minute.'

'Well, don't hang about. Put the body in one of the bins.'

The shorter man ran off towards the gym. The tall man turned his attention back to Jamie.

'Well, boy, you've not been straight with us. I don't like that.'

Jamie gulped and tried to think. The plan he had formed back in the squash court could still be used. But he would have to change it. And quickly.

'Money,' he blurted. 'I –'

'I don't want your money. You haven't got any money. At least, not the kind of money I might be interested in.'

'Money for the girl. The … the money she owes you.'

The man looked him over. 'What about it?'

'I've got it. I ... I was going to come and find you tomorrow and tell you. I've ... I've ... got it saved up ... for her ... I mean and ... I could... get it for you and give it to you and ...'

The hand at his neck tightened and he choked. The man snarled at him.

'You haven't got any money. Why should I listen to you? I haven't got time for this.' He glanced at the knife fondly. Jamie spluttered on frantically.

'I ... inherited it. And I've been saving. It was for something else. But I met the girl and she ... she told me she owed you some money –'

'A lot of money. A hell of a lot of money.'

'Yes and ... and I decided to help her and pay you off so you'd ... you'd leave her alone again.'

The grip on his neck eased slightly. Jamie studied the face before him, praying that the man's greed would overcome his desire to kill. There was a sound of footsteps and the shorter man reappeared.

'There's no sign of her,' he said. 'And there's no hole in the fence by the gym either.' He glanced at Jamie, then back at his companion. 'Haven't you done him yet?'

The taller man still looked at Jamie.

'Not yet,' he said quietly. 'But I'm going to lose my patience pretty quick if he doesn't tell us where the girl is now.'

Thoughts rushed through Jamie's mind. He knew his life depended on the answers he gave these men. And the girl's life, too, perhaps. He kept his eyes on the taller man.

'I made it up about the hole in the fence by the gym. To distract you. To give her time to get away. She'll be gone by now.'

'Which way?'

'There's a hole in the fence just along from the main gate.' He felt the grip round his neck tighten and hurried on, choking. 'No, there ... there really is a hole. I'll show you if you like. I ... I wanted to give her time to get away. She'll have ... escaped by now.'

▷ **13** *by scruff of sb's neck:* roughly holding to the back of sb.'s neck **24** *settle up with sb.:* give sb. what they are owed **31** *straight:* honest **32** *gulp:* swallow hard because of fear **43** *choke:* be unable to breathe **46** *fondly:* with love · *splutter:* speak quickly and with difficulty **48** *inherit sth.:* receive sth. from sb. when they die · *save:* keep money instead of spending it **54** *greed:* strong desire for more possessions **65** *make sth. up:* invent sth. (esp. a story) · *distract sb.:* take sb.'s attention away from sth.else

The grip eased once more. The taller man stood back, then, without warning, flung the knife. Jamie gasped – but the knife was not aimed at him. It flew past his face and thudded into the door of the lab, where it quivered and then was still.

The man watched it for a moment, then went on.

'Well, Jamie, it looks like you'll have to pay the price yourself. We want the girl and we want the money. Instead, we've got you and you've got the money. So let's start with the money. You say you've got it. Well, the first thing you can do is give it to us.'

'I haven't got it on me.'

'I wasn't thinking you had it on you.' The man leaned closer. 'It's a lot of money. Little boys don't carry that kind of money around with them. But I expect you to get it by tonight. Now, just so we understand each other.'

The man's hand swung out. Jamie felt the fist smash into the side of his face.He fell backwards against the building. Another fist drove into his stomach, forcing out the breath. He doubled up, gasping for air.

Another blow came, to the side of his head, knocking him down, then a boot crashed into the small of his back. He writhed over the ground, moaning with pain. A hand seized him by the hair and twisted his head round. He looked up into the tall man's eyes, as chilly as the night sky that shrouded them. The voice that spoke was chillier still.

'I don't like people who cross me, Jamie. So I make sure they understand what's what. Now, today you're going to get hold of this money, and you're going to bring it to me in my car. The money will be in cash inside an envelope. Of course, you won't be stupid enough to phone the police or tell anyone because you've probably realized by now that I'm not a very nice person and we wouldn't like to see a series of unfortunate accidents, starting with your mother, and then your father, and maybe that nice boy you walk to school with. And perhaps he's got some brothers and sisters. And then, of course, the girl, not to mention yourself.'

He paused.

'Don't forget yourself. Because there won't be any escape, Jamie. And don't think getting us caught will solve any problems for you because it won't. Firstly, we won't both be in the car, so my friend here will be free to hunt you down, and secondly, even if we did get caught and go to prison, we've got plenty of friends who'll be happy to do jobs for us on the outside. You'd be watching your back every minute of the day and night. Am I making myself clear?'

Jamie looked at him dumbly, too shocked to speak.

The hand whipped out again and smacked into his cheek.

'Am I making myself clear?'

'Yes.' Jamie swallowed hard. 'Yes. Where ... where do I meet you?'

The man thought for a moment.

'You go to the roundabout where the ring road joins up with the motorway. Just down from it, there's a lay-by. I'll be pulled in there. You come on your own. At six o'clock.'

Jamie stiffened. Of all the places to meet, of all the times to meet.

'I ... I'm not sure I can get out there by six o'clock. Couldn't I meet you in town somewhere? Maybe at –'

'You meet me at the lay-by. Six o'clock. And don't be late.'

Jamie opened his mouth to speak again but there was no time for further protestation. He felt himself lifted from the ground and thrown against the side of the lab. The man advanced, pulled the knife from the door, and seized him by the hair again.

'Don't let me down, Jamie.'

'I'll ... I'll be there. And if I give you the money, will you ... will you leave the girl alone after that?'

The man's eyes bored into him like darts.

'We'll think about that when we've seen the money.'

The fist flew out again and Jamie remembered no more.

When he came to, the men had gone. He was lying on the ground beside the Chemistry lab, shivering in the cold, his head aching where the blows had struck. He felt his cheeks and nose. Nothing seemed to be broken though he was badly bruised. But he knew he'd been lucky. Their first plan had been to kill him.

He struggled to his feet and looked about him. It was still dark and the men seemed to have gone but he was wary now. They had clearly

▷ **2** *fling – flung – flung sth.:* throw sth. with force **20** *the small of sb's back:* the lower part of the back where it curves in · *writhe* [raɪð]: twist or move your body because you are in great pain **23** *shroud sth.:* cover or hide sth. **25** *cross sb.* (infml): betray sb. **43** *dumb:* unable to speak **54** *lay-by:* area at the side of the road where vehicles may stop for a short time **62** *bore into sb./sth.:* stare in a way that makes sb. feel uncomfortable **68** *be bruised:* Quetschungen/Prellungen haben

not been fooled earlier when he and the girl had been inside the squash court. They must have parked the car down the lane, walked back and climbed the fence or used the gap, and waited for them to appear again.

He looked at his watch. Five o'clock. A couple more hours and his parents would be waking. Waking to find him gone. But they seemed like inhabitants of another world now.

He stumbled towards the main building, still watching for signs of the men. The bins came into view and he walked slowly towards them, trying not to show any interest in them, in case he was being watched. He stopped by the one in which he had left the girl, and looked about him again.

Still he saw no one.

He made up his mind and pulled up the lid.

She was not there.

He closed it again and leaned on the bin, unsure whether to feel relieved or concerned. He knew he had to find her at the roundabout before the men did. But there was much to do first. And despite the pain, hunger and cold, he somehow had to will himself into action.

He wandered down to the squash court, found his rucksack still lying on the ground and wearily picked it up. Then he crossed the playing field, squeezed through the hole in the fence and made his way slowly and painfully down the lane.

SEVENTEEN

If it had been anyone else but Spider, the sight of a figure climbing in through his bedroom window and leaning over the bed might have provoked at least a gasp. But he merely stared in silence for a moment, then murmured, 'What the hell are you doing here?'

Jamie sat on the bed, trying to calm himself. He was so tense now he felt his nerves would snap. Spider sat up in bed and switched on the lamp.

'Christ, what happened to you? Who did that to your face?'

Jamie looked away, unable to speak. Spider started to climb out of bed.

'I'll get Mum and Dad.'

'No.' Jamie reached out and held his arm. 'Please. They mustn't know anything. You see, I've...' He stopped, breathing hard.

'Take your time,' said Spider.

'I've ... I've left home.'

'You've what?'

'I've left home.' The words tumbled out, now that he had started. 'I left last night. My parents probably don't know yet, unless they've already woken up. But they never wake before seven. And I didn't see a light on. So they ... they probably don't know anything yet.' He looked away towards the window. 'They didn't hear me put the ladder up against your wall.' He laughed nervously. 'You must be the only person in the country who sleeps with the window ajar when it's as cold as this.'

▷ **29** *snap:* break **40** *tumble out:* come out quickly and uncontrolled

He knew he was talking aimlessly but his thoughts were no longer his own. Spider spoke at last.

'But why? I mean, I know things are difficult. But running away's surely a bit drastic. Did you have a bust up or something?'

Jamie frowned. There was so much Spider didn't know and it was unfair to get him involved in all this without telling him everything. But the less he knew, the better. Then, if he was asked questions, he couldn't give anything away. Yet something had to be said, especially in view of what Jamie was about to ask him.

'I did have a bust up with my dad. He knocked me about and ... well, anyway, I've just got to get away. So I'm hitching up north this evening – with a friend.'

'Who?'

'Don't ask me.' He saw the concern on Spider's face and hurried on. 'Please don't ask me. The less you know, the better.'

'But you're in trouble. Anyone can see that. Can you at least tell me who did that to your face? Was it your dad?'

'No. It was ... someone else.'

Jamie sighed. If he mentioned the two men, Spider would put two and two together and connect him with the girl. He remembered what the taller man had said about hurting Spider's family, and the thought of Amy and Becky in the hands of those men decided him. He shook his head.

'It's best you don't know anything. Please don't try and force me. If anyone asks, you haven't seen me, right? And you mustn't call the police. You don't know anything. It's for your own good.' He took a deep breath. 'But there's something else. I ... I need your help. I need it really badly.'

Spider drew his knees up to his chest.

'What do you want me to do?'

Jamie studied his friend's face in the glow of the lamp.

It was so still, so composed, so strong. He had been dreading this moment.

'I don't know how to ask you this. But there's no one else I can turn to. I can't turn to my dad or my mum. But this ...' He hesitated, anxious to give no clues about the girl. 'This friend of mine's in much bigger trouble than I am. If I don't do something, this ... person ... could get killed.'

He paused again, waiting for Spider to speak. But his friend was silent. He looked down and went on.

'I need ... money. A lot of money. It's not for myself. It's for my friend. It's to pay off the ... the people who are after my friend.'

He stopped, still looking down at the bed. Spider spoke.

'How much do you need?'

Jamie looked up at him, desperately trying to think of something to say other than what he had to say. But there was nothing else.

'I need ... as much as it costs to buy a good sports car.'

Spider held his eyes for a long time, then leant back against the head of the bed.

'When do you need it?'

'I'll pay you back. Somehow. It'll take time but –'

'When do you need it?'

Spider's voice was quiet, almost detached. Jamie took another deep breath.

'Today.'

Spider's eyes flickered away for a moment, then back.

'I can't get it to you until after school. And it might be a bit difficult reaching you without someone spotting us. I mean, your parents will call the police the moment they find you're missing. And it'll get round the school, and other people will be looking out for you. And people are bound to ask me questions and watch what I'm doing. Where will I find you?'

Jamie tried to think. At the moment he was still stunned at the calm, unquestioning attitude of his friend. It seemed inconceivable that Spider could face the prospect of losing everything he had worked so hard for without some show of anger. Jamie almost wanted him to be angry. He touched his friend on the arm.

'I'm so sorry. I'm so sorry. I'll –'

'Never mind that. Where will I find you?'

He forced himself to think. He certainly should keep Spider away from the roundabout by the ring road. Then he thought of the obvious place.

▷ **4** *bust up* (n) (infml): serious quarrel **32** *composed:* gefasst · *dread sth.* [dred]: be very afraid of sth. **53** *detached:* showing no feeling **61** *bound to do sth.:* certain or likely to do sth. **63** *stunned:* surprised and shocked **64** *inconceivable* [ˌɪnkən'siːvəbl]: impossible to imagine or believe **65** *prospect:* possibility that sth. will happen

'You know the little alleyway by the health food shop? Can you meet me in there? I'll be right at the end, where it bends round out of sight.'

'Are you sure you want to meet there? You get a lot of drifters hanging about that place.'

Jamie frowned. 'Shadows,' he murmured.

'What?' said Spider.

But Jamie shook his head. 'It doesn't matter. I'll meet you in the alleyway. I'll be all right.'

'I won't be able to get the money to you before about five.'

'That's OK. I can meet you at five.'

'I suppose it's got to be in cash?'

Jamie stared at him, again feeling the enormity of what he was asking.

'Yeah. In an envelope. Christ, I'm so sorry. What will you say when people ask you if you've seen me?'

'I'll just say I haven't.'

'What about the money?'

'What about it?'

'Aren't you mad at me?'

'Yep.'

There was no anger in Spider's voice. But Jamie knew what the loss of this money would mean to his friend.

'What about the car you were going to buy? What'll you tell your parents?'

'I'll tell them it's not quite what I want after all and that I'm not going to rush into buying anything.'

Jamie looked down. 'I feel a bastard.'

'You're not a bastard. You're just a pain.' Spider swung himself out of bed. 'Have you eaten anything?'

'Not much.'

'Have you got any food on you?'

'No.'

'Money?'

'No.'

Spider's face softened.

'You'd better stay here while I sneak downstairs. I'll see what I can rustle up.'

Spider slipped out of the room and closed the door behind him.

Jamie waited, listening for sounds from his own house next door, but there were none. After what seemed a long while the door opened again and Spider entered with a plastic bag. He closed the door behind him and sat on the bed.

'Get these inside you.'

He pushed some sandwiches into Jamie's hand and Jamie attacked them gratefully. Spider watched him for a moment, then went on.

'Listen, I haven't taken too much food, just some rolls and cake, and some apples. If I take too much, Mum and Dad'll notice and when I'm asked questions, it'll be obvious I've seen you and helped you. It'd be far better if you could buy yourself something.' Spider reached into the drawer of his bedside cabinet. 'Here's some money. It's not much but it'll get you and your friend enough food for a day or two. And I'll bring you more tonight.'

Jamie looked up from the sandwich, guilt flooding over him once more.

'Take it,' said Spider, then, when Jamie still hesitated, reached out and pushed the notes into Jamie's pocket. 'Listen, buy the food early today, before the news really gets out about you. And don't go anywhere where people know you. Try somewhere where you can slip in, buy the food and slip out quickly. What about that mini-market just past the bus station? Do you ever go in there?'

'No.'

'Well, try there. With any luck, the only person you'll see will be some sleepy cashier. Where are you going to hang out today?'

'I don't know.'

'Well, you need to make sure no one sees you. No one at all, if possible, not just police and people who know you. You don't want some do-gooder seeing your boyish, youthful appearance and asking why you're not in school. Not that you look very boyish and youthful right now. Hang on.'

Spider crept out of the room again but quickly returned.

'Lean forward,' he said.

'What's that stuff?'

▷ **4** *drifter:* person who moves from one place to another with no real purpose **13** *enormity:* fact of sth. being very serious **38** *rustle sth. up* (infml): find or make sth. quickly **54** *guilt:* Schuldgefühle **67** *hang on* (infml): wait a minute

'Arnica cream. Mum swears by it. We only have to bang an elbow and she's slapping it all over us.'

He squeezed some cream from the tube and reached out. The touch of his finger on the bruises made Jamie wince, but he said nothing and continued eating the sandwiches. Spider went over all the bruises, then leant back.

'It's the best I can do. Here, take the cream and put some more on later.'

'Thanks.'

Spider glanced at the bedside clock, then back. And for some moments simply watched him eat. Then he spoke again.

'Are you sure there's no other way out of this?'

And Jamie looked back at him; and shook his head.

'I wish there was,' he said.

Spider was right about the mini-market. The only person who took any notice of him was the girl at the check-out and she merely asked him for the money. He had already decided that his best place to hide was the alleyway itself. Uncomfortable though it was, and too close to the town centre for comfort, there seemed little point in moving about from place to place. The more he moved, the more likely he was to be spotted.

It was cold, though, and damp as he huddled against the wall. He was not left to himself. A stream of motorbike riders came and went as usual, parking their bikes under the sheltered part of the alley, but only a few came far enough down to see him at the end and none approached him. He looked away when they appeared.

There were tramps, too, who ambled down the alleyway, seeking to rest there perhaps, but they retreated at the sight of him. Only one person bothered him, an old drunk who lurched over him, spitting and moaning, before stumbling away back to the street.

There was no sign of the police, nor any pursuit. Eventually darkness fell and it grew colder. And with the cold came the greater chill of fear.

Just after five, he heard footsteps in the passageway.

EIGHTEEN

It was Spider.

His friend dropped a carrier bag on the ground.

'I can't stay long. There's a big hue and cry about you and everybody's suspicious of me. I don't think I was followed but I'm sure Mum and Dad think I know something. We had your dad on the doorstep first thing this morning, asking if I'd seen you.'

Jamie shifted restlessly. It would be touch and go to reach the roundabout by six and he was anxious to be moving – but he had to know more.

'What was he ... what was he like?'

'Your dad? Bit rude when he turned up this morning. He was more civil after school but he looked nervous. The police were no problem to deal with.'

'The police?'

Spider looked at him. 'What did you expect? They've been in school, asking questions.'

'Have you ...' He hesitated. 'Have you seen my mum?'

Spider shook his head. 'Your dad looked bad enough so I expect she's worse. You didn't leave a note, your dad said, so for all they know, you could be dead.'

'I should have written them one. I wish I had now.'

Spider reached inside his bag.

'I thought you might say that so I brought you some paper and an envelope. I'll post it. I'm not putting it through the letter box – I might

▷ **27** *amble:* walk at a slow relaxed speed **28** *retreat* (v): move away or back **31** *pursuit* [pəˈsjuːt]: act of searching for sb. **37** *hue and cry:* general outcry about sth. **41** *touch and go* (infml): uncertain if sth. will be successful

be spotted. I've put a stamp on it. If you send it from here, they might think from the postmark that you're still in the area.'

Jamie looked at him gratefully. Spider had been so practical, so unselfish.

'I'll make this up to you,' he said.

'You certainly will,' said Spider. 'Go on. Write the thing and get moving. I can't stay long.'

'What excuse did you give your parents for slipping out?'

'I didn't give an excuse. They're at the supermarket with the twins but they'll all be back soon so hurry up. And here's the money. I had a couple of hundred left in the account so I shoved that in, too. Hope it helps.'

Without ceremony, Spider pushed an envelope towards him. Jamie stared at it.

'Go on,' said Spider. 'Take it.'

Jamie took the envelope and thrust it inside his rucksack. Spider handed him a piece of paper, a pen, and an envelope with a stamp on it.

'Use my back,' he said, and turned round.

Jamie rested the paper against Spider's back and tried to think of what to write. But it was difficult. He wanted to tell them he wasn't dead, so that they didn't start a murder hunt, but he also wanted to say something that would make Mum feel better.

He wasn't sure he had anything to say to Dad.

'Hurry up,' said Spider. 'I've really got to be moving. I don't want to have to tell more lies to Mum and Dad. And don't print the letters. You need to make sure your parents recognize the handwriting.'

Jamie started to scribble. He didn't say much, partly because there wasn't time, partly because the point of the pen kept pushing through the paper; but mostly because he really didn't know what to say.

He wasn't happy with the result and it seemed a little melodramatic but it was the best he could do.

I'm OK. Don't worry about me. But I can't see you any more. I'm going away to live my own life. Please don't try to find me. I won't come back.
I'm sorry.
Jamie

'Finished?' said Spider.

'Yes.' He sealed the note inside the envelope.

Spider turned round.

'If you address the envelope, I'll post it on the way back.' Spider glanced at his watch. 'Quarter-past five. I'll drop it through the box at the depot in King Street. It'll catch the last post and your parents should get it in the morning.'

'Can you turn round again?'

Spider turned round and Jamie wrote the address on the envelope. 'OK.'

Spider turned back and took the envelope.

'I bought some more food for you on the way here. It's in the bag.'

Jamie looked at him.

'Thanks. Thanks for everything. I'll never forget what you've done for me.'

And Spider looked back, the familiar half-smile on his face; then, without a word, he reached out, cuffed Jamie lightly over the head, and left.

Jamie watched him go, his mind in a turmoil of guilt and fear. But it was time to act. He stuffed the food that Spider had brought inside his rucksack along with the food he had bought himself. Then he noticed the envelope.

He pulled it out, looked warily about him, and opened it.

It was all there, including the two hundred pounds extra as Spider had said. He stared at it all. Thousands of pounds, each note a fragment of his friend's dream, now gone.

But perhaps they would save a girl's life.

He separated the two hundred pounds, put them in his pocket and counted the rest again to make sure the amount was right. Then he replaced the notes in the envelope, pushed it inside his rucksack and fastened the catch, and set off towards the street.

He had planned his route during the hours of waiting.

Down the main street – that couldn't be avoided – then along Litchfield Avenue as far as the traffic lights where it should be

▷ **5** *make sth.up to sb.:* do a good deed to sb. for sth. good they have done to you **28** *scribble sth.:* write sth. quickly and carelessly **48** *familiar:* well known **49** *cuff sb.:* hit sb. quickly and lightly in a playful way **51** *turmoil:* state of confusion

possible to cut through one of the lanes that straggled up to the ring road. But he would have to hurry. He was really late now.

He forced himself to walk down the main street but kept to the side and hugged the shops. The town was crowded with people flooding out of work, not to mention pupils from the school, and he knew this was the most risky stretch. He kept his head down and pulled his hood up.

He reached Litchfield Avenue safely and turned down it, relieved to be away from the main street, but now self-control deserted him. He started to run, the rucksack thumping up and down on his back. He had to get away from this part of the town. He knew so many pupils who lived round here.

He reached the traffic lights at the bottom and waited for the signal to cross. To his right, he sensed someone's presence beside him. He turned away and readjusted his hood.

'Too cold to be standing around,' said a voice.

He pretended not to hear. It wasn't a voice he recognized but that meant nothing. It might still be someone who knew him. Or a policeman. The voice spoke again.

'Murphy's law, isn't it? They're always on red when you want them on green.'

He made himself glance round and saw an elderly man standing there. The man caught his eye and winked.

'Running away from home?'

'What?'

The man nodded at Jamie's rucksack.

'That's fairly bulging. You look like you're stocked up for a long trip or maybe you've just got the Crown Jewels in there.'

Jamie looked at him suspiciously and said nothing. The man smiled.

'It's time.'

'What?'

The man smiled again, apparently unconcerned at the abrupt response he was getting.

'The lights.'

'Oh.'

They crossed together and parted company on the other side. Jamie forced himself not to run straight away but let the man disappear in the direction of the sweet shop, then he sped off again.

He had a choice of lanes before him, all leading the way he wanted to go. Frantically he ran his mind over the people he knew who lived round here, but there were so many, it scarcely made any difference.

He cut through Parkhurst Lane into Campton Drive and on to the parade of shops at the end. So far, so good. There were only a few people on the streets here and none of them seemed interested in him as he ghosted by in the darkness. He gave the shops plenty of room and skirted round the other side of the street as far as the entrance to Channock Hill.

Still no one called his name; no car pulled over. He ran up Channock Hill and turned down Pendle Lane towards the ring road. Now, far ahead, he could see the lights of the traffic moving along the ring road towards the motorway junction. Nearly ten to six. He might just make it but it was going to be close.

He raced on, keeping his eyes alert. The garden centre appeared on his left, then, a hundred yards on, the playing fields opened up to the right, and beyond them, raised on the embankment, the ring road itself, cluttered with lorries and cars.

He ran to where Pendle Lane crossed under the ring road, climbed over the fence and scampered up the bank to the top. This was the next dangerous moment. The road was so much used that anyone might see him and recognize him. And if there had been reports on the news about him, even strangers might guess who he was.

But he had to take that risk.

He plunged on down the road, the traffic thundering past him. He felt exhausted now, and it was still nearly half a mile to the lay-by at the motorway junction. Somehow he drove himself on, cursing the weight of the rucksack, and starting to panic about the man he was to face.

The road started to bend to the right and now, as he drew closer, he could see the roundabout ahead and the motorway running over it,

▷ **1** *straggle:* spread in different directions **4** *hug sth.:* (here) keep close to sth. **6** *stretch:* area of land **20** *Murphy's law:* humorous rule that if anything can possibly go wrong it will go wrong **27** *bulge:* (here) be unusually full and rounded **41** *run one's mind over sth.:* go through (a list of) sth. in one's mind **44** *parade:* (here) row **47** *skirt round sth.:* go round the edge of sth. **52** *junction:* place where two or more roads etc. meet **57** *cluttered with:* full of **59** *scamper:* move quickly with short light steps · *bank:* Böschung

and there, too, the flyover under which the girl was waiting, he hoped, hidden in a forest of stone.

But his eyes did not linger on this. They were scanning the road ahead. And there, just a short distance from him, was the lay-by.

In it was a car.

He stopped and caught his breath. The man mustn't see him running – if it was the man. It was hard to tell. He strained his eyes to see as the headlights from passing vehicles brushed over the car, but it was no good.

He walked slowly forward, trying to think of some way to give himself a chance of safety. And suddenly an idea came. It wasn't a very good one – indeed, it might misfire by arousing the man's anger – but it was all he could think of right now.

A lorry rumbled past and threw its beam over the car in the lay-by.

And in that moment Jamie caught the outline of the man he feared.

NINETEEN

He didn't knock at the window but stood there, a few feet back from the passenger door. The man saw him and a moment later the automatic window slid down.

'Get in.'

Jamie looked at the face, remembering what the man could do. He also wondered where the shorter man was hidden. There was no sign of him here but that meant nothing. He opened the passenger door and leaned down.

The man glanced at him.

'I'm not talking to you standing out there.'

Jamie took a deep breath, climbed slowly into the car and closed the door behind him. Without a word, the man started the engine.

Jamie forced himself to speak as confidently as he could.

'If you drive me anywhere, you won't see the money.'

The man looked him over coldly.

'What?'

Jamie clenched his fists. He knew he must not let the man drive him away. All his instincts told him that any journey with this man would be the last he ever made.

'If you drive me anywhere, you won't see the money.'

'Don't play games with me, boy.'

'I'm not … playing games. But …' Jamie moved back slightly, aware of the anger building in the man's eyes. 'I haven't got all the money on

▷ **12** *misfire:* fail to have the intended effect · *arouse sth.:* cause sth. **15** *catch the outline of sb./sth.:* suddenly see the shape of sb./sth.

me here. I left half of it just down the road. It's only a few yards away. I'll tell you where it is when you promise me you'll leave the girl alone and let me out of the car safely.'

The man studied his face for a few moments, his features dark and threatening, then, without switching off the engine, held out his hand.

'Money.'

Jamie felt his hands tremble but somehow managed to look the man squarely in the face.

'When you've promised to leave the girl alone. And me.'

The man raised an eyebrow, reached forward and turned off the engine. Then, with startling suddenness, he seized Jamie by the throat and thrust his head back against the window of the door.

'Ah!' Jamie cried out with the pain. The man jerked him forward by the hair, then rammed his head back against the window. Jamie squirmed in the seat, trying to shake his head free, but the man was too strong. Again and again his head was yanked forward, then driven back against the window.

Suddenly he was released but the man's face moved closer.

'Now listen, Jamie.' The voice seemed to breathe venom. 'You're not in a position to make conditions. And let's be honest about this – how do you know I'd keep any promise I might make? Much as I'm flattered to have your trust, I'm not sure I'd even trust myself. No, Jamie, the problem you've got is that I might just get angry and kill you here, instead of where I was planning, take what money you've got on you, go and look for the rest and, even if I find it, keep on looking for the girl until I find her and kill her, too. She won't get very far. Her trail's warm enough. Besides, even if you could trust me to keep my words, you haven't thought of my mate. Now he really is a nasty piece of work. I wouldn't bet on him honouring a pledge.'

The man looked him over in silence for a moment, then gave a chilly smile.

'So we'll look at what money you've got and then we'll talk again.'

Jamie knew it was foolish to resist. And what this man said was true: his word would count for nothing. There was little else for it to pay up and hope.

'I'll give you what I've got,' he said.

The man leaned back but stayed close enough to make Jamie feel uncomfortable. Jamie hesitated, then opened his rucksack and drew out the notes.

Once more the enormity of what he was doing overwhelmed him. Spider's hard-earned money given away to a man like this, who might well take it and still go on hunting the girl. But there was just a hope that the money would take away the lust for blood. He had to cling to that.

He held out the notes.

The man took them and counted them.

'So where's the rest?'

'Let me get out of the car first.'

The man eyed him in silence, and seemed to be pondering what to do. Clearly he was unwilling to lose Jamie and wanted him dead, but he must want the rest of the money, too. Jamie tried to think of some way of putting pressure on him.

'If you let me out of the car and don't bother me or the girl again, I'll tell you where the rest of the money is and ... and I won't tell the police about the video.'

The man frowned. 'What video?'

'The video of you and your mate.'

The man sneered at him.

'You haven't got any video.'

'It's not mine,' said Jamie, thinking hard. 'It was taken by the parent of one of the girls at my school.'

The man looked at him, disbelieving yet suspicious. Jamie hurried on.

'When you talked to me outside the school gate that time, there was a netball match going on. One of the parents took some video film of his daughter playing. He told me about it because he said I was in the picture, talking to two men. I haven't seen it but you'll be on it.'

He knew this was a tissue of lies but he prayed the man would not suspect it. More ideas rushed into his head and he blurted them out.

▷ **4** *features:* Gesichtszüge **8** *squarely:* directly **11** *seize sth.* [si:z]: take hold of sth. · *throat:* front part of the neck **13** *jerk sb. forward:* make sb. move forward with a sudden, short movement **15** *squirm:* move around a lot making small twisting movements because you are uncomfortable **28–29** *nasty piece of work* (infml): very cruel person **52** *put pressure on sb.:* try to force sb. to do sth. **58** *sneer* (v): show that you have no respect for sb. by the expression on your face or the way you speak **69** *tissue of lies:* a story that is full of lies

'And the headmaster saw you. He came out after you'd gone and asked me who you were. He'd been watching you through the window of his office. He said he thought you looked suspicious. And people in town have been talking about you asking them about the girl and giving them a phone number to ring and saying you'll pay them money and stuff.'

'None of that incriminates me.'

Jamie tried to think. He knew this was not evidence but it was just possible that he'd said enough to make the man feel it would be best to take the money and clear out. He bit his lip and spoke again.

'If you leave me and the girl alone, I promise I won't mention you to anyone or say anything about all this.,'

He paused, then added: 'And unlike you and your mate, I do keep my word.'

The man looked him over in silence. Jamie tried to stare boldly back, but it was hard. The eyes frightened him so much. There was no mistaking how dangerous this man could be.

Suddenly he spoke. 'Get out of the car.'

Jamie needed no second invitation. He opened the door and jumped out, pulling the rucksack after him. The thunder of the traffic broke upon his ears again but it was a welcome sound. The man jumped out of the driver's door.

'Where's the rest of the money?'

Jamie pointed back down the carriageway.

'About fifty yards down that way. Just back from the road where the fence posts get taller there's a gate with a big stone nearby. I put the money under the stone. It's in an envelope.'

The man pointed a finger at him. 'You wait here till I get back.'

'The money's there.'

'It better be.'

The man's face had changed suddenly. All the coolness was gone; in its place was the flame of greed. Jamie said nothing. He knew he should run – he wanted desperately to run – but he knew, too, that he had to wait, not because he'd been told to but because he had to see this man drive away, with the money.

The man hurried off down the carriageway.

Jamie moved back from the car to give himself more room to escape but there was no need. The man was soon back in the driver's seat, counting the rest of the money.

The next moment, the car was gone.

Jamie waited for a few minutes to see if it reappeared but there was no sign of it or the other man. He looked about him a few more times, then crossed the carriageway, made his way to the other side of the roundabout, and walked towards the flyover.

▷ **7** *incriminate sb.:* make it seem as if sb. has done sth. wrong or illegal **15** *bold:* brave and confident

TWENTY

The noise of the traffic seemed even louder here. He stood by the slip-road to the motorway, checked around him one more time for signs of danger, then climbed up the verge.

It was just as she had said. The road fell away below him and as he drew closer to the underside of the motorway, he could see that the concrete supports created a kind of flat pocket, bordered by slabs. He reached the outer slab, a low horizontal wall, and looked over it into the dark space within.

At the far end was a figure, bent over the opposite side.

He heard a moan, just audible over the roar of the traffic, then the figure moved and he caught the profile of the girl. Suddenly she fell against the slab.

He clambered into the little space, hurried up behind her and put a hand on her shoulder. She jumped.

'Easy,' he said. 'It's me.'

She turned towards him and he saw her face twisted with pain. He shook his head in despair.

'What have they done to you? How did they get to you?'

She stared at him for a moment, then grimaced and clutched her stomach.

'Don't be stupid. I'm ... having a bloody baby, you idiot.' She moaned again. 'God, two weeks early. Why couldn't it wait till I got to Cumbria? I started to feel funny this morning, then it ... cleared a bit so I ... came out here about twelve to rest and wait for you and ... and suddenly it started.'

He took a step back.

'I'm going for an ambulance.'

'No!' She gripped his arm. 'Please don't go.'

'But –'

'Please.' Her face was pleading, desperate, her hand still tight round his arm. 'It's going to come soon and … I'm really scared.'

'But you need a doctor. I don't know what to do.'

She held him tighter still. 'Don't leave me alone here.'

He saw the fear in her face and knew he could not go. She had already endured six hours of solitary labour in this miserable place but now, with darkness fallen and the worst part surely to come, he knew he had to stay and try to help her. If he could master his own fear.

He took her hand. 'I'll stay.'

He saw the gratitude in her eyes but there was no time for her to answer as her body tensed in another spasm. She bent over the slab, groaning. He let go her hand and put his arm round her shoulder.

'It'll be OK,' he said.

She didn't answer and merely went on groaning, then, after a while, the pain seemed to ease. She slumped to the ground, her back against the wall, her eyes fixed ahead of her.

'Are you cold?' he said.

'Yes.'

'Have you still got that blanket you were carrying with you?'

'In my holdall.'

He fetched the blanket and draped it over her shoulders. She looked up at him, shivering. She seemed so vulnerable, yet somehow so beautiful. The spasms soon started once more and the cycle of pain and relief went on, the contractions growing steadily more stressful.

An hour passed. The contractions grew stronger, more frequent, the girl shifting position constantly as she tried to ease her discomfort. Jamie watched, mopping her brow with his handkerchief and trying to offer words of encouragement, but feeling increasingly helpless. Suddenly she gave a moan, struggled into a squatting position and gripped him by the shoulders.

▷ **10** *moan* (n): loud deep sound expressing unhappiness or suffering · *audible:* able to be heard · *roar* (n): loud continuous noise **13** *clamber:* climb with difficulty **35** *endure sth.:* experience and deal with sth. painful · *solitary:* lonely, being alone · *labour:* the process of giving birth to a baby **40** *spasm:* sudden and painful tightening of muscles **41** *groan* (v): make a long deep sound because you are in pain **54** *contraction:* Geburtswehe **58** *squat* (v): sit on your heels with your knees bent up close to your body

'Help … me!' she said.

He put his hands on her waist and held her steady.

'Come on,' he said. 'You're nearly there.'

She started to scream, her hands digging into his shoulders so hard he wanted to cry out, too. He watched in horror, remembering stories he'd heard of women who died in childbirth. Then he looked down.

The top of the head had appeared.

'It's coming,' he said. 'It's coming.'

The girl didn't look down and merely gripped him as before, breathing hard.

'Come on,' he said. 'Push!'

And she pushed, screaming as before and gripping him more tightly than ever. Suddenly, with a gasp of relief, she slumped against him.

He held her for a while, then slowly leaned back enough to glance down.

The head was out now but not the body. He looked back at the girl. She was still breathing hard and her head now rested on his shoulder, as though she wanted to sleep.

'Come on,' he said. 'One more effort.'

And sure enough, with the next contraction, the body eased out.

He reached down and put a hand under it. It felt slippery and strange; tiny, yet somehow immense. And it was crying.

The girl seemed unable to speak, unable to move. He looked back at her.

'I've got the baby. It's OK.'

She said nothing and simply clung to him, gulping in air as the baby went on crying. He waited, wondering why she hadn't reached down to take the child. Then, suddenly, she gave a moan.

And he felt the baby slip free.

He moved back, still holding it, then recoiled at the sight of what had come out with it. The girl spoke at last, her voice so weary he could barely hear it.

'It's the afterbirth. We'll sort it out later. Just give me my baby.'

He lifted the baby towards her, his eyes still on the unpleasant-looking jelly at the end of the umbilical cord. The girl took the child in her arms and cradled it. Making soothing noises as it cried. Then she looked at Jamie.

'Didn't you check?'

He stared at her, then realized what she meant. She gave a tired laugh.

'I've got a little boy. I've always wanted a little boy.'

She undid her shirt and put the baby's mouth to her breast.

'He won't get any milk just yet. Dear little boy.'

He said nothing, feeling strangely redundant and still uneasy about the afterbirth. The girl slumped back against the slab, holding the baby to her.

She was spent.

Jamie watched her for a moment, trying to think of something he could do. Then he saw that the blanket had slipped to the ground. He picked it up and draped it over her again.

'Thanks,' she said, wrapping it quickly round the baby, too.

Her eyes were glazed with weariness but at least the baby was now silent and seemed to be trying to suckle. Jamie moved closer.

'What do we do now?' he said.

She took a long time answering, as though it were a struggle even to speak.

'We've got to clean him and dress him before he freezes to death. And we've got to get rid of the umbilical cord and the afterbirth.'

Jamie looked down at it again. 'How do we do that?'

She took some deep breaths, then slowly sat up straight. 'I know what some peasant women do. I've read about it. But I don't know if I can –' She stopped, still breathing hard. 'Can you pass me my holdall? I've got some things in there I've been collecting for the baby.'

'What, like nappies?'

'And baby clothes.'

He handed her the holdall and she pulled out some string. Then she looked round at him.

'I'd ... rather do this bit on my own. If I can bring myself to.'

'Are you sure?'

▷ **23** *tiny:* very small **31** *recoil:* move your body quickly away from sb./sth. because you find it/them frightening **36** *umbilical cord:* Nabelschnur **37** *cradle sb.:* hold sb. gently in your arms · *soothing:* intended to make sb. feel calm **43** *undo sth.:* open sth. (e.g. buttons) that is fastened or tied up **45** *redundant:* (here) not needed or useful **48** *spent* (infml): very tired **54** *suckle:* drink milk from a mother's breast **62** *peasant* ['peznt]: poor farmer working a little piece of land **66** *nappy:* Windel

'Yeah, I think so. Anyway, I need to … clean myself up a bit.'

She looked at him somewhat shyly but he understood well enough. He jumped to his feet.

'I'll be over there. Just shout if you want me.'

He walked over to the outer slab and gazed down at the roundabout, blowing his hands in the cold air. Below him cars passed in the darkness like weird anonymous lights, some heading for the motorway, others along the ring road, some back towards Ashingford. And he found his mind running with them, to Mum, to Dad, to what he had left behind.

He gave the girl plenty of time, then cautiously looked round. She had straightened her clothing and was now lying with her back to the far wall, the baby still wrapped up inside the blanket and held to her breast.

He walked over to her and knelt beside her. 'Are you OK?'

She looked up. 'I'm … not very comfortable, but I'll be all right. We must get the baby dressed before the cold gets to him. Can you help me?'

'Sure.'

He edged closer. 'Did you … get rid of the afterbirth?'

'Yes.'

He hesitated. 'What did you do?'

'I bit through the cord and tied the end with string.'

He stared at her, slightly shocked. 'So where's –?'

'I've thrown it away.'

Jamie frowned. 'Didn't it hurt him?'

She looked down and he saw this was not the time to throw questions at her. He quickly forced a laugh.

'Well, he looks fine, anyway, just like his mum. Come on. Let's get him dressed.'

The girl paused for a moment, as though she were having to will herself to move, then she reached inside the holdall, pulled out some wipes and some cotton wool, and started to clean the baby.

'I'll get his clothes out,' said Jamie.

He poked inside the holdall and found a little baby suit with mittens, trousers and hood, and some boots, socks, a vest, a shirt, and a tiny hat. The girl pulled a nappy from the holdall, then suddenly stopped.

'Are you all right?' said Jamie.

She didn't answer, didn't look up. Her face was dark with fatigue. He reached out and took the nappy from her.

'Come on,' he said. 'I've seen the way they do this.'

But she took the nappy back again.

'I'll do it,' she said.

In the end they both did it, with considerable fumbling, first the nappy, then the clothes. The girl leaned back against the wall, holding the baby to her, wrapped once again inside the blanket. Jamie watched her for a moment, then rummaged in his rucksack for the sandwiches he had bought and handed her one. She took it with a nod of thanks, still holding the baby, and they lay back together against the slab and ate in silence.

He waited until she had finished eating before he spoke.

'I paid the men.'

She looked round at him. 'What?'

'I paid the men. At least, I paid the taller one. Just before I turned up here. I got caught by them after I left you in the bin at school. They –'

She gripped his arm, stopping him.

'What did they do to you?'

'It's OK. I'm all right.'

'But what happened?'

'The tall guy beat me up. But I told them I'd give them the money if they promised to leave you alone. I know a promise from them isn't worth much but I thought it might make a difference.'

'But you didn't give them any money?' A look of incredulity passed over her face. He thought of Spider and frowned.

'I've got a friend.' He bit his lip. 'A bloody good friend. He's been saving up for –' He stopped. There was no point going into details. It would only make the girl feel guilty and he didn't want that. 'He lent me the money. Enough to pay off the men. I met the tall guy just down the road from here and gave it to him.'

'Where was the other man?'

'I don't know. Didn't see him. Just gave the tall man the money and he drove off.'

▷ **7** *weird* [wɪəd]: strange **33** *wipes*: tissues used for cleaning skin **36** *mittens*: Fausthandschuhe **40** *fatigue* [fə'tiːg]: extreme tiredness **65** *incredulity* [ˌɪnkrə'djuːləti]: unwillingness or inability to believe sth.

She stared at him for some time, not speaking. Then he realized she was crying.

He hesitated, then slid an arm round her shoulder, ready to pull it back the moment she gave any sign that she didn't want it; but she moved forward, as if to help him, and he pulled her gently towards him. She leaned her head into the crook of his neck, still clasping the baby to her.

'I'm sorry ... I don't mean to ... She sniffed. 'It's just that ... no one's ever shown me so much ...'

He stroked her arm.

'It's OK. Don't worry. We're in this together. I help you. You help me.'

'I don't help you. How do I help you?'

He thought for a moment, anxious not to say the wrong thing. There was so much that she gave him, so much that he knew he could not express, partly because he didn't understand it very well himself. He knew he was captivated by the warmth and softness of her body, the tickle of her hair under his nose, her scent, her voice, but much more than all this, he was drawn to the enigma of what she was.

He fumbled for words that would not offend her.

'You help me because ... because I'm on my own, like you, and I ... don't know what I'm going to do or where I'm going to go. And you've become a ... kind of a friend.' He turned his head away but still felt hers against him. 'I really ... care about you.'

He was making a complete mess of this. He fell silent, feeling useless and clumsy, and certain that he had now spoiled the tender atmosphere they had had a moment ago.

But she moved her head towards him, making him turn and look at her, then leaned forward and kissed him softly on the mouth.

'Thank you,' she said.

And she turned back to the baby once more.

Somehow they slept, despite the cold, the girl rolled over on her side, hugging the baby to her, Jamie lying against her back, his arm flopped over them both; and the blanket draped over them all.

Some time later he woke to the sound of the baby crying. Darkness was still around them and so was the sound of the traffic, though it was intermittent now. The cold was growing worse.

He felt the girl stir and start to unbutton her shirt. His arm was still over her and she made no effort to push it away, but he pulled it back and spoke.

'How are you feeling?'

'I've been warmer.'

Jamie looked over at the baby. 'What about him?'

She pulled the baby to her breast. 'I think he just wants a bit of this.'

Gradually the crying ceased. Jamie watched, feeling slightly embarrassed, then he thought of something.

'What are you going to call him?'

The girl was silent for a while. Then she turned and looked at him. 'What's your name?'

He stared at her, remembering what they had agreed about questions. But so much had changed now.

'Jamie,' he said.

She turned back to the baby and kissed it. 'We'll call him Jamie, then.'

His mouth fell open. She had said it in such a matter-of-fact way it took him by surprise. It was some moments before he realized he should be flattered. But there was another gift he wanted from her. And one he now felt he was owed.

'What's your name?'

She was still looking at the baby. But she answered at once. 'Abby.'

And that was all. No more details, no more questions.

But it was a name. And the knowledge of it now seemed the most precious thing he had.

▷ **17** *captivate sb.:* (here) attract sb. **19** *enigma* [ɪ'nɪgmə]: person, thing or situation that is mysterious and difficult to understand **25** *make a mess of sth.:* not do sth. very well **26** *clumsy:* doing things in an awkward way **37** *intermittent:* not regular **55** *matter-of-fact:* sachlich **63** *precious* ['preʃəs]: rare and worth a lot

TWENTY-ONE

At around three in the morning, she spoke again. 'I can't sleep in this cold and I'm worried about little Jamie. We're better off moving.'

He stretched and rubbed his eyes.

'Whereabouts in Cumbria is it we've got to go?'

'A few miles from ... I think it's called Cartmel Fell. I've got the address somewhere.'

'And these people ...'

'I've never met them. I told you, they're friends of a friend. But they've been told I'm coming and they said I can stay.' She seemed to sense his anxiety. 'I'm sure they won't turn you away. Not if you've come that far with me. But I can't ask them until we get there because they're not on the phone.'

He looked away, thinking over the other anxieties that were now preying upon him. She seemed to sense those, too.

'Listen, you don't have to come with me. If you want to go back home and sort out whatever's wrong –'

He shook his head firmly.

'I'm coming to Cumbria. I want to. Anyway, I'm not leaving you after you've just had a baby.'

She looked at him for a moment, then smiled. 'Let's go, then.'

They emptied out the rucksack and stuffed the contents into the holdall, then Abby changed the baby's nappy, wrapped him in the blanket again and placed him upright inside the rucksack; then, keeping a hand under his neck for support, she slid her arms – first one, then the other – through the straps and pulled the rucksack into her body so that the baby was facing her chest, her hand still behind his neck; and they set off down to the slip-road that led up to the motorway.

Jamie watched her closely. She was walking very gingerly, her face set with determination, and she clearly didn't want him fussing over her, but he could see she was in great discomfort.

They reached the slip-road and Jamie turned to face the traffic, his hand held out to start hitch-hiking. Abby came up to him.

'I'll do it,' she said. 'They're more likely to stop if they just see a girl on her own. You go and sit over there with the baby. And try and keep well back so the headlights don't pick you up so easily.'

'But you should be sitting down, not me.'

'I can't help that. I've got to stand so they see me.'

She looked at him. 'Go on, Jamie, just do it. I'll sit down if I get really tired.' She moved closer so that he could take the rucksack. 'And keep a hand under his neck. Don't take it away, whatever you do. He's got to have something supporting his head.'

Reluctantly, he took the baby from her and, holding the rucksack as she had done, moved back from the road. A tense hour went by as he sat on the verge, the baby – mercifully still sleeping – close against his chest, and watched Abby standing by the roadside, her arm outstretched. He noticed her body swaying as she fought with exhaustion. At last a transit van pulled over.

She opened the door and started talking to the driver.

Jamie hurried over with the baby. Inside the van was a dumpy man with a somewhat bleary expression, who looked at him with some surprise.

'Oh, there's two of you. Didn't see.'

'Is that OK?' said Abby.

The man didn't look too happy but he shrugged.

'I can't take you all the way but I can give you a start and drop you off at a motorway exit or a service station.'

'That's fine,' said Abby and made to get in.

Jamie stepped forward.

'I'll go in the middle. Here, take the rucksack.'

▷ **10** *anxiety* [æŋ'zaɪəti]: state of feeling nervous or worried that sth. bad is going to happen **30** *fuss over sb.:* pay a lot of attention to sb. **45** *mercifully:* luckily **48** *transit van:* Lieferwagen **50** *dumpy:* short and fat **51** *bleary:* not able to see clearly esp. because you are tired

He didn't know why he was being cautious. This man looked no threat but for some reason he didn't want Abby sitting next to him. Abby said nothing but took the rucksack and let him climb in first.

'It's a bit of a mess,' said the man. 'Just kick those bits of piping out of the way or shove them behind you.'

Jamie climbed in and pushed the piping to the side. Abby sat down beside him, placed the rucksack carefully on her lap, one arm over it, the other under the baby's head, then leaned wearily against him. The driver watched uneasily.

'You didn't say you had a baby.'

'Sorry,' said Abby.

The man now looked distinctly uncomfortable, as though he'd bitten off more than he'd intended to chew in picking them up, but he started to drive on.

'Hope it's not a noisy baby.'

'He'll be quiet,' said Abby. 'He's very sleepy.'

'I know the feeling. I'm Alan, by the way.'

'Im Sarah,' said Abby, 'This is Tom.'

'What's the baby called?'

'Steven.'

Jamie looked at Abby and saw she was fighting to keep awake. He hoped the driver wouldn't ask too many questions; but the man spoke again at once.

'So what do you do, Tom?'

Jamie didn't answer, forgetting for the moment who he was meant to be. Then he felt Abby nudge him.

'Er ... I'm ... a student.'

'What are you studying?'

'I'm ... sort of ... between courses.'

'What does that mean?'

Abby looked round at the man. 'He's dropped out. To marry me.'

The man guffawed. 'Oh, I get it.' He glanced at the baby again. 'Shotgun wedding. So you're married?'

'We're getting married,' she said.

'You look a bit young. How old are you both?'

'Eighteen.'

The man yawned suddenly.

'Well, I wish you well. I got married when I was twenty and I thought that was young but I suppose I didn't have a kid to think about then.' He shook his head. 'I've had four of them to think about since.' He yawned again. 'Don't mind me rambling on. I picked you up to stop me falling asleep. I've been driving all night and I've got to keep going for another few hours so if you can talk to me, it'll help.'

So they talked to him, or rather Jamie talked. He knew Abby was aching for sleep and, tired though he was and anxious in case he said something that might give them away, he knew he had to give her the chance to rest.

And so, while she rested, he forced himself into conversation, mostly probing the man with questions about his life and family, and, when questioned himself, inventing a fantasy life that included Abby and the baby. And, as he talked, he found himself wishing it were true.

But the life he was describing – that pleasant, dream life – was not his life, nor was it hers. Their lives still hung in the balance of uncertainty. And one thing was growing in his mind as the miles passed behind them.

He was running away. Running from a problem he had not resolved to a future that could not resolve it.

Finally, it seemed, the man fell silent. Jamie looked round at Abby. She was slumped against him, her head on his shoulder, her arms cradling the rucksack with the baby inside, sleeping as soundly as his mother. Jamie closed his eyes and dozed, too.

Some time later he heard a voice. It was the radio.

'The news at six o'clock. Police are still looking for a sixteen-year-old boy who has disappeared from his home in Ashingford. Jamie Williams was last seen ...'

He opened his eyes and looked towards Abby but she was still sleeping, and so was the baby. He glanced to the right.

The man seemed uninterested in the news bulletin and soon fiddled with the radio until he found some music. Jamie yawned and tried to sleep again.

▷ **4** *piping:* Rohre **5** *shove sth.* [ʃʌv]: push sth. **13** *bite off more than you intend to (*usu. *can) chew:* get yourself into a more difficult situation than you had intended **26** *nudge sb.:* push sb. gently esp. with your elbow to get their attention **31** *drop out:* leave school, college without finishing your studies **32** *guffaw* [gəˈfɔː]: laugh noisily **33** *shotgun wedding* (infml, old-fashioned): wedding that has to take place quickly because the woman is pregnant **41** *ramble on:* talk about unimportant things for a long time **45** *ache for sth.* [eɪk] (infml): have a strong desire for sth. **49** *probe sb.:* find out about sb.

But his thoughts were racing now, not northwards to where his body travelled, but back, always back, to the spectre of his former life.

The man dropped them at a motorway service station and they used some of Spider's money to buy breakfast. Abby seemed only slightly refreshed from her sleep and was still walking uncomfortably, but she was eager to push on. They changed the baby's nappy and made their way to the motorway slip-road.

An hour later they were moving again, this time with a lorry driver who also wanted conversation and who received from Jamie much the same story as the previous driver. But this man only took them forty miles. They waited again and soon picked up a lift with some students in a camper van who shared food with them, asked no questions at all, and took them another twenty miles.

More waits, more lifts. Rain started, stopped, started, stopped. By ten in the evening they were heading through the lanes of Cumbria with a forester and his son in a battered Land Rover. By midnight they were standing at a deserted country crossroads.

Abby was exhausted.

Jamie looked at her. He, too, was tired but he knew his weariness was nothing compared with hers. And they would surely have to walk now, with little chance of picking up any more lifts out here.

He glanced down at the baby, asleep in the rucksack he was now cradling to his chest. It felt so strange to be carrying a child. He walked over to Abby and reached down for the holdall she had dropped to the ground.

'Let me take that,' he said.

She looked up at him. 'Jamie, I don't know if I can go any further.'

'How far is it from here?'

She pulled a slip of paper from her jacket pocket and squinted at it in the darkness, then peered up at the signpost.

'About eight miles from here. We go down this road for five miles, then take a right fork and after a while we should come to a farm and then a lane that takes us to the house.' She leaned wearily against the signpost. 'But I don't know how much energy I've got left.'

He put his arm round her.

'Listen, we'll take it really slowly and we'll stop for rests whenever we want, but we've got to make it. And we're going to make it. For the baby's sake.'

She took a deep breath. 'So are you up to a hike?' she said.

He looked at her, trying to hide his dread at the prospect of an eight-mile walk, and even managed a smile.

'I didn't have any other plans for tonight.'

▷ **16** *forester:* a person who works in the woods · *battered:* old and looking worn out **17** *deserted:* empty of people **29** *squint* (v): look with your eyes partly shut to see better **30** *peer* (v): look intently **39** *be up to sth.:* (here) be ready/able to do sth. · *hike* (n): long walk in the country **40** *dread* [dred]: feeling of great fear · *prospect of sth.:* Aussicht auf etwas

TWENTY TWO

The walk through the night seemed endless. They spoke little, just a few words now and then, and mostly to ask if the other was all right.

He offered to carry the baby and the holdall but Abby refused and insisted on taking the baby, which soon started to cry. They stopped and changed his nappy by the side of the lane, then trudged on through the night.

As the hours passed, the air grew colder.

Jamie looked at Abby. Her head was down and she was moving more and more slowly, as though every step were a struggle. But at last they reached the fork.

Jamie looked round at her.

'Turn right here?'

'Yes.'

'How far is it to the lane that leads to the house?'

'Don't know. Just hope it's not too far.'

But an hour later they still had not reached it. They forced themselves on for another half an hour, then finally saw a cluster of barns to the right.

'If that's the farm,' she said, 'the lane should be just past it.'

'Has it got a name, this farm?'

'Yes, but I can't remember it.' She stared at the slip of paper. 'Can't read this. It's too dark.'

'Let me have a look.'

She handed him the paper and he studied it.

'Looks like … Beck … Beck …'

'Beckside Farm. I remember it now.'

'Well, let's see if it is.'

They wandered past the barns and saw more buildings and what looked like the entrance to the farm. A dog started barking within. Jamie went over to the gate and peered at the notice.

'Beckside Farm. That's it. Come on, let's move on before they think we're burglars.'

They left the farm behind them and walked on. Half a mile down the road was a small notice pointing down a lane.

Abby walked over and read the words aloud. 'To Mill Dam Lodge.'

'Is that the place?'

She nodded.

'OK,' said Jamie. 'One last haul and we're there.'

But the last haul was the toughest of the night, and by the time they came to the end of the lane and saw the huge house with its barns and outbuildings, Jamie was carrying both the baby and the holdall and it was five o'clock in the morning.

There were no lights on in the house.

Abby leaned against the door.

'Doesn't seem right to wake them at this hour but I can't stand up any longer.'

And she pressed the bell.

It seemed to make no sound and Jamie wondered for a moment whether it was working. Then, through the glass panel in the door, he saw a light go on inside the house and, a moment later, the outline of a figure descending the stairs.

The front door opened and a woman appeared in a night-dress.

She looked about fifty and was tall and well-built, with strong, capable hands. She studied them calmly, as though being woken at five in the morning were the most natural thing in the world.

'Can I help you?'

It was a pleasing voice, Jamie decided, certainly not the voice of an enemy, but he let Abby do the talking.

'I've been given your address. I'm sorry we've turned up at this time of the morning.'

The woman shrugged. 'Happens all the time.'

▷ **5** *trudge:* walk slowly and with heavy steps because you are tired **17** *cluster:* group of things close together **18** *barn:* Scheune **32** *burglar:* person who enters a building illegally in order to steal **38** *haul* (n): distance that needs to be travelled **49** *panel* ['pænl]: flat surface

Suddenly she looked hard at Abby. 'You wouldn't by any chance be ... Jude's friend?'

'Yes.'

'Abby?'

'Yes.'

The woman smiled. 'We've been expecting you for days. We were getting worried something had happened to you. But we thought you were on your own.'

'This is Jamie.'

'Hello, Jamie.'

'Hello.'

The woman's eyes looked him over in the same calm way. He had the impression that there was very little that could startle this woman. Her eyes left him and moved to the rucksack he was holding to his chest.

'So that's ...' She peeped over the top at the baby, who was sleeping soundly inside. 'That's three of you. Are there any other members of the party I need to know about?'

'I'm sorry,' said Abby. 'I would have warned you but you're not on the phone, are you?'

The woman smiled again. 'Fortunately not. We're not very keen on telephones here. Anyway, my name's Savita. Come inside.'

She led the way into the house, switching on lights as she walked through the rooms. Jamie looked about him, too dazed to take much in, but he saw that everything was clean and simple, and there was a pleasant air of comfort about the place.

Savita entered the kitchen and turned to face them. 'Right. Food, wash, or sleep first?'

Jamie looked at Abby and they spoke in unison. 'Food, please.'

'OK.' Savita glanced at the baby who was still fast asleep inside the rucksack. 'No point in taking him out of there just yet. He looks so comfortable. But let's put some cushions under him.'

She found some cushions and made a kind of bed at the end of the kitchen table. Jamie laid the baby carefully down, then slumped into a chair. Abby did the same and they sat there in silence.

Savita started cooking and before long a smell of toast, mushrooms, and baked beans was wafting towards them. Soon they were eating ravenously. Savita put two mugs of tea on the table.

'I'll go and fix your room,' she said, and disappeared.

Jamie glanced at Abby. 'The room … she thinks we're …'

Abby looked up. 'Don't leave me, Jamie.'

She held his gaze, as though seeking reassurance. He felt slightly embarrassed, but managed a smile.

'Of course I won't leave you. Not if you don't want me to.'

She smiled back, but it was a tired smile, a vulnerable smile.

Savita soon returned.

'The room's ready. More food for anyone?'

They shook their heads.

'Right,' said Savita. 'Let's go, then.'

She led the way out of the kitchen and up the stairs. Abby carried the sleeping baby and Jamie came last, wondering about this place. Clearly it was some kind of sanctuary, as Abby had said, but they would surely have to pay to stay here.

They reached the first floor, made their way along a corridor and up more stairs to the second floor, then along another corridor to the end and into a large bedroom.

'There's a basin over there,' said Savita. 'The loo's down the corridor and the bathroom next to it. If you need me, I'm in the first room at the top of the stairs on the first floor. Sleep as long as you want.'

And, with a brief smile, she left them.

Jamie looked around the room, still feeling awkward about the sleeping arrangements. There were two single beds but he noticed they had been pushed together and made up as one. He wondered whether he should offer to move them apart again.

But Abby seemed unconcerned about this. She placed the baby on the bed, then simply pulled off her jacket, jumper, shirt, skirt, and socks and dropped them to the floor. Then she eased the baby out of the rucksack and, cradling him in her arms, climbed into bed.

'Put the light out, Jamie. Hurry up.'

Somewhat flustered he switched off the light and stripped down to his underpants in the darkness, then felt his way round to the other side of the bed. At least the room was warm. He would have no need of pyjamas. He found the other side of the bed, pulled back the sheet and climbed in.

▷ **24** *dazed:* unable to think clearly, esp. due to shock, etc. **29** *in unison* ['juːnɪsn]: together **37** *waft* [wɒft]: come through the air **57** *basin* ['beɪsn]: Becken **71** *flustered:* nervous and confused

Abby had turned towards him, the baby held close to her so that he was lying between them, and she already seemed to be drifting into sleep. But she murmured: 'Goodnight.'

'Goodnight,' he said.

Tired though he was, he did not find sleep mastering him at once. He found this strange, considering how much he had yearned for sleeep throughout the course of the day, especially during the long walk through the night. But now all he could think of was the closeness of Abby and her child.

Both were sleeping, the little boy turned inward to his mother's breast, while she ...

He studied her face in the darkness.

It seemed full of mystery. And there was a scent about her, not the scent of the road, which she no doubt couldn't wait to wash off, but another scent: a scent so intimately part of her that he yearned just to lie here and drink it like wine. She had never been so beautiful to him as she was now.

In that thought, he finally slipped into sleep.

Some time later, he felt her hand on his. He woke and saw light breaking through the windows of the room, though it was only the pale light of early morning. She had not opened her eyes, had not shifted her position, and the baby was still tucked in between them. But she pulled his hand gently towards her and placed it over her shoulder, then let go.

She did not speak, did not look at him, seemed still deep in sleep. He moved a little closer to her, to make himself more comfortable now that his arm was outstretched. She shifted, too, just a little towards him. He breathed hard, drinking in the scent of her again, enjoying the softness of her skin under his hand. The little baby was close against his chest and he found himself curiously captivated by it.

And they slept on, all three.

TWENTY THREE

The next time he woke was to the sound of the baby crying. He opened his eyes to see broad daylight at the window and Abby sitting in the chair, putting the baby to her breast. Her hair was wet and she had a towel wrapped round it. To his surprise, she was wearing different clothes: a navy-blue skirt and a pale blue shirt.

He sat up in bed and she looked round at him.

'Hi,' she said. 'Savita gave me the clothes and she said she'll try and get hold of some men's things for you if you want. These don't quite fit but it's the first time I've worn anything else for ages. What do you think?'

'They look great.'

'It feels so good to have a shower and a hair-wash. Why don't you have one? There's shampoo and soap in the bathroom which Savita said we could use, and she's given us a couple of new toothbrushes and some towels.' Abby turned and murmured to the baby. 'And she's got lots of nice things for you, too, hasn't she? Yes, she has. Yes, she has.' She kissed the top of the baby's head.

Jamie watched, a little uncomfortable at the baby talk and still feeling self-conscious about being dressed only in his underpants and sharing a bed with Abby. But he needed a shower and couldn't lie here for ever. He pulled back the top-sheet, hoping Abby would continue to watch the baby. But she looked round again.

▷ **13** *scent* [sent]: pleasant smell **15** *intimate* ['ɪntɪmət]: private and personal **46** *murmur* (v): speak softly **50** *self-conscious:* nervous or embarrassed about your appearance or what other people think of you

'I've had a long chat with Savita. She said Savita's not her real name.'

'What is?'

'I don't know. She didn't tell me. She said she changed her name to symbolize her break with the past. All the women here have got a past.'

'Is it only women here?'

She nodded. 'Apart from you. Who's a lucky boy, then?'

He frowned, thinking not of this but of his own past, which was now reaching out to him again.

Abby chuckled. 'Don't worry. You're not going to be thrown out. Savita's accepted us as an item. She thinks you're Jamie's father.'

'What else did she tell you?'

'She just said her old life was so painful she'd decided to start again. So she gave herself a new name and came here. She inherited a lot of money and bought the house and land outright, and decided to use it as a refuge for women in trouble.'

'When did she come here?'

'Twenty years ago.'

'And the women … I mean, do they live here all the time?'

Abby shook her head.

'Only a few of them. Most are just passing through like me. It's not an official home or anything. It's a kind of commune. Savita's made it her life's work. She lets people stay for a while, until they can get back on their feet, then they move on and others take their place. They don't have to pay anything but they're asked to make a donation if they can and everyone's expected to muck in and work. They've got animals and they grow their own vegetables and stuff.'

He looked down. 'So you'll … you'll have to move on, too.'

'I always knew I would.'

He thought once more of his own life, and the mess he had still not resolved; and then of his feelings for Abby. Feelings he had never had before; feelings that bound him to this place.

She came round, still holding the baby to her, and sat next to him on the bed.

'Don't stay just because of me, Jamie. If you've got to go back, I understand. When I ran away from home, I thought I was escaping, but all I was doing was running away from myself. I should have stayed and fought my corner.'

He looked at her. 'Are you saying it's always wrong to run away?'

'No, not always. Everybody's situation's different. Some people are in danger if they stay, and they have to run.'

'What happened to you? I mean –'

He stopped, remembering what they had said about not forcing questions. But, to his surprise, she started to talk.

'I ran away to get away from my dad. I just couldn't handle things any more. I took as much money as I could find from his wallet and Mum's purse and walked out of the house in the middle of the night.'

'How old were you?'

'Fourteen.' She sighed. 'I was a total mess. I didn't know what to do, where to go. All I knew was I didn't want to go back home. So I left the area and wandered about, sleeping rough, getting hungry, cold. Then I met Angelo.'

'Angelo?'

A look of pain crossed her face.

'The taller one.'

Somehow he'd guessed and he was starting to guess the rest, though he hoped he'd be wrong. She studied his face for a moment with an air of concern, as though anxious not to hurt him.

'Go on,' he said. 'Please. If you can bring yourself to tell me.'

She glanced at the baby for a moment, then kissed its head and looked back.

'He found me when I was at my most vulnerable. I had no money, no food, nowhere to live. He took me in, looked after me. He was good to me in the beginning. And he was a real charmer. I fell for him hook, line and sinker. I thought he loved me. I can't believe I was so stupid.'

She frowned. 'He didn't love me. He just wanted me for one thing and when he got bored with that, he decided to use me for something else.'

Jamie drew breath. 'You mean …?'

She narrowed her eyes. 'Some men make money honourably and some get other people to make it for them. You understand?'

▷ **12** *be an item* (infml): be a couple **16** *outright:* (here) immediately and without a mortgage (= Hypothek) **26** *donation:* gift of money, food clothes, etc. **27** *muck in* (infml): help with the housework **39** *fight your corner:* defend yourself **65** *charmer:* person who behaves in an agreeable way to make others like him or her · *fall for sb.:* fall in love with sb. **66** *hook, line and sinker* (infml): completely

He saw anger in her eyes, as though all the pain of her past had flooded back in this confession of her life. His own life slipped into focus, and he saw it for what it was. And it was nothing compared to this.

He spoke as gently as he could. 'And … the baby?'

'It's his,' she said bluntly.

He stared at her, and the defiance and hurt in her face made him lower his eyes.

'And the money he wanted from you?'

'It was money I'd earned for him, and it was only part of what I made for him. He didn't want to lose me. He threatened me. Told me if I ran away, he'd always find me and make sure I never worked again, not for him or anyone else. And he said he'd make sure no man ever found me attractive again. He meant it, too.' She shuddered. 'I saw what he did to Jude and some of the other girls.'

She fell silent again and looked down at the baby, as though she drew strength from it. Jamie waited for a moment, unwilling to press for further confidences. She looked up again.

'The money wasn't for me. It was for Jude. To help her get away.'

'What happened?'

'He beat her up so badly. I knew I had to help her and try to escape myself. Angelo kept lots of cash at his house so he didn't have to declare it, but I knew where he hid it so I broke in and took it. Gave most of it to Jude so she could get away to Canada and start a new life. She's got people out there she knows.'

'Why didn't you go with her?'

'I had some stupid idea I wanted to sort things out with my family.'

'So who's the other man? The stockier one.'

Abby's face curled up in disgust.

'That's Vittorio, Angelo's brother. They're half-Italian, half-English. Vittorio's even more dangerous than Angelo. They're always at each other's throats. Neither trusts the other. They're always fighting about something.'

'But what made you come to my part of the country?'

'To see my dad. We're from Leeds originally. But after I ran away from home, I found out from a friend that my family had moved down to Ashingford. When I ran away from Angelo, I was desperate. I'd only kept a little bit of money for myself because I wanted Jude to have a good chance of making it, and what I had I soon spent on food and stuff. I thought about going straight to Cumbria but I knew Angelo would be after me, and Vittorio would be with him to make sure his brother didn't get the money and then pretend he'd never seen me, so I decided to swallow my pride and go home and ask Dad to help me pay off Angelo.'

She looked down.

'I watched the house for days, trying to pluck up courage to ring the doorbell, and getting more and more scared because by this time I'd seen Angelo and Vittorio in town.'

'So what happened?'

'I forced myself to call at the house.' She looked up at him. 'The day we met in the alleyway by the health food shop.'

'And what did your dad say?'

'He wouldn't even look at me. I stood on the doorstep and tried to speak to him. He just stared past me, said he didn't have a daughter any more because I'd walked out, told me my brother was carrying the family's hopes, said if I'd got into trouble, that was my fault and I'd have to sort it out myself.'

'Bastard. Sorry, I mean –'

'It's OK. You're right. He is a bastard. I'll never see him again now.'

'But what about your mum?'

'She wasn't there when I called but she wouldn't have made a fuss. She never argues with my dad.'

Jamie frowned, disturbed at the echoes from his own life. He looked at her.

'Abby – look, don't answer this if you don't want to, but – what did your father do to you to make you want to run away?'

She looked away.

'He ignored me.' She wiped the corner of her eyes. 'He ignored me from the day I was born. It was like I didn't exist. I tried to make him love me but he took no notice of me because he was so busy loving my brother.'

Jamie stared at her. 'How old's your brother?'

'Same age as me. He's my twin.'

▷ **23** *declare sth.:* inform the tax authorities how much of sth. (esp. money) you have earned **27** *sort sth. out* (infml): get sth. resolved or settled **43** *swallow your pride:* do sth. which you don't want to and which makes you feel bad **46** *pluck up courage to do sth.:* make yourself do sth. though you are afraid to do it

'But why did your father love him and not you?'

'Because I'm not a winner at anything. My dad only likes winners.'

He reached out and touched her arm.

'Abby, you are a winner. As far as I'm concerned.'

'Thanks.' She smiled at him. 'But my dad wouldn't agree with you.'

Jamie frowned. 'So ... what is it your brother's a winner at?'

Abby looked down and kissed the baby. 'Danny's big thing has always been squash.'

TWENTY FOUR

Over the next few days Jamie tried to come to terms with what Abby had told him, but all he felt was anger.

Not at Abby. Never that. She was dearer to him than ever now. His anger had other targets and he knew what he had to do.

He did not speak of this to Abby or tell her of his own life and his encounters with her brother and father. She needed to grow strong again, not carry his emotions on top of hers. And she was growing stronger. Day by day the healing effect of Savita and the others was starting to show.

He was glad for her.

There was a bond between the women that he knew he could not share but it didn't matter. All that mattered was Abby. So he peeled potatoes and washed up and chopped wood, and spoke when others spoke to him, and wandered round the farm, thinking, waiting; and at night he lay down with Abby, and they talked together, and then slept, the baby now beside the bed in a little makeshift cot.

The week drew on. It was growing colder again and the days were short. It was hard to believe Christmas was so close. On the Thursday evening after supper he wandered into the fields alone and gazed up at the night sky, and stayed there until it was late.

▷ **9** *come to terms with sth.:* accept sth. unpleasant by learning to deal with it **12** *target:* particular thing or person that something is aimed at **14** *encounter* (n): meeting (usu. unpleasant) **24** *makeshift:* used temporarily for a particular purpose · *cot:* a small bed for a baby

When he returned to their room, the light was off and Abby was already in bed, the baby asleep in the cot. He walked round to his side of the bed, stripped down to his underpants, and climbed in.

Abby lay still, but he knew she was not sleeping. After a while she spoke.

'You're leaving in the morning, aren't you?'

He rolled over and looked at her. She was lying on her back, staring up at the ceiling and did not turn his way. She spoke again.

'I know you've got to go back to sort out what's wrong. Whatever it is.'

'I don't want to. I want to stay with you.'

'I want you to stay with me. But ...' She turned to face him, her eyes bright, in spite of the darkness. 'I can feel your restlessness.' She watched him for a moment.

'We've got different paths, Jamie. I've got to stay here for a while, if Savita will let me, then I'll have to move on, too.'

'Back to your family?'

'No, never. That's over.'

She was silent for a long time. Then she spoke once more.

'Jamie?'

'Yes?'

'Hold me.'

He reached out his arm and stretched it over her shoulder and down her back. And, to his surprise, felt only bare skin. She moved towards him and lay against him, her head against his chest.

He tensed slightly, embarrassed by her nakedness and his feeling of arousal. She reached over his side and stroked his back. He turned his head to look down at her and found her looking up at him.

They kissed, softly, on the mouth, and drew back; then kissed again, a longer kiss but still soft, still hesitant; then a third kiss, longer still, but always soft, always hesitant, as though each were asking permission of the other. Suddenly she drew back and he saw she was crying.

'Abby, what is it?'

She dipped her head into his chest and went on crying.

'Abby, please. Is it something I've done?'

She shook her head, but still wouldn't look up.

He stroked her hair, feeling desperately confused and somehow guilty. Then Abby looked up.

'It's not you, Jamie. It's me. Don't you see? I've ... I've been damaged. I can't ... make love with you or anything. It's not that I don't want you. It's just that I've ... I've been messed with so much I don't know if I'm –' She gulped. 'I haven't got any protection and even if I did, I'd never forgive myself if I gave you –'

'Abby –'

'I mean, I'm going to get myself checked out as soon as I can, and little Jamie, obviously, in case he's picked up any ... you know ...'

'Abby, it's OK.'

'But it's not just that. I mean, I can't even ... kiss you without feeling ... kind of ... screwed up inside. And now you'll think I'm playing with your feelings and you'll hate me and –'

'Sssh, Abby. It's OK. I'm never going to hate you.'

He kissed the top of her head as she went on crying against his chest. 'We don't have to do anything. We can just lie here. I never thought we were going to make love.' He tried to sound self-mocking. 'I don't suppose I'd be much good at it anyway. I'd probably stick the wrong thing in the wrong place.'

She didn't speak, but she was still crying, though more softly. He went on, still stroking her hair.

'We don't have to do anything. It's good just ... just to hold you. I've never held anyone before. Not someone naked, I mean. And your body's so beautiful.'

'No one's ever told me my body's beautiful, no one who meant it, anyway. Angelo used to say I was sexy.'

'You are sexy.'

'But he was just flattering me to make me do what he wanted. He didn't really mean it.'

'I mean it.'

'I'm glad you do.'

They lay in silence for a moment. Then Jamie looked down at her.

'Abby?'

'Yes?'

'I understand you not wanting to make love. But why does it make you feel funny to kiss me?' He tried the self-mocking tone again. 'But

▷ **27** *arousal:* Erregung **41** *damaged* ['dæmɪdʒd]: hurt badly **42** *mess with sb.:* treat sb. badly **50** *screwed up* (sl): confused, upset **66** *flatter sb.:* say nice things about sb., usu. because you want sth. from them

break it to me gently. I know I'm not much of an expert in that department.'

She turned her face towards him, her eyes close to his, and he saw a look of tenderness there.

'Jamie, you should have more confidence in yourself. There's nothing wrong with you in that or any other department.'

She shook her head. 'It's not you. It's just that …' She thought for a moment. 'When you kiss someone, mouth to mouth, it's one of the most intimate things you can do with them. It opens you up to them. That's not a problem if you're together in yourself but if you're screwed up, it really –'

She broke off, still staring into his eyes. He thought she was about to cry again and reached out a hand to stroke her cheek.

'Abby' he murmured. 'Abby.'

And she leaned forward and kissed him again, on the mouth, still softly as before, and he kissed her back, as gently as he could, frightened lest he kiss too hard and cause her pain, but her own kiss grew stronger and she slid her hand round the back of his neck and pulled him to her. He felt her body tight against his, her breasts moving softly against his chest. Then, slowly, she pulled back, and looked into his face again, and he saw she was crying once more.

'Abby, I'm sorry. I didn't mean to –'

But she reached out and put a finger on his lips. 'It's OK. I promise it's not you.'

She wiped her eyes with the back of her arm. He watched for a moment, then reached out a hand and with a finger smoothed away the moisture from her cheeks. She took the hand in hers, then, still holding it, twisted over on to her side, and pulled his arm over her so that he was snuggling into her back; and they lay there together in the darkness.

'Jamie?'

'Um?'

'Thanks.'

'There's nothing to thank me for. I should be thanking you.'

'What for? What have I done for you?'

He thought for a moment, anxious not to say the wrong thing, but also anxious not to think too long in case she thought he was having to make something up.

'You've made me believe in myself again,' he said finally.

He felt her squeeze his hand. Silence fell once more, a long silence this time, and he thought for a moment she was drifting into sleep. Then …

'Jamie?'

'Um?'

'When you leave … don't say goodbye.'

He drew back to look at her but she spoke at once.

'Don't pull back. Hold me.'

He leaned closer again and pressed his face into her hair. 'No goodbyes?'

'No. Just go.'

'Like a shadow?'

She breathed slowly in; and slowly out again. 'Yes. Like a shadow.'

He thought for a moment. 'And is that all we'll be now? Shadows?'

She twisted her face round and peered at him in the darkness.

'Whenever you see your shadow, Jamie, just remember you're looking at me.'

▷ **1–2** *in that department:* with regard to that, in that area **26** *smoothe sth. away:* make sth. disappear by rubbing softly **27** *moisture:* wetness

TWENTY FIVE

Mum and Dad were nowhere to be found.

He walked down the hall and checked the sitting room, then made his way through to the kitchen, and then upstairs, and back down again.

The house was empty.

And there was something eerie about it.

It was immaculately tidy. There was no rubbish in the bins; nothing was out of place. Surfaces had been scrubbed or polished or waxed; taps gleamed; ornaments had been dusted and replaced. The books in the shelves had been rearranged into near-perfect symmetry.

It was as though no one lived here.

Not that tidiness was unusual. Mum was fastidious and had always kept things neat and clean. But this was different. And why the house should be empty at half-past seven in the morning he could not understand.

He sat down at the kitchen table and thought back over the last twenty-four hours. It had been a tough journey, walking, waiting, picking up lifts where he could; then getting stuck at midnight for three hours until the lorry driver picked him up and brought him the last of the way.

He had pictured so many variations of this homecoming and all of them involved confrontation with Dad, yet here he was, sitting in an empty house.

No matter. There were other confrontations he had returned for and they would not wait.

But first he had to eat.

He pulled open the fridge. Here, at least, were signs that someone lived here. It was full to bursting. Mum must have gone shopping last night. Out of curiosity, he opened the freezer.

That, too, was full-up, and he noticed Mum had left lots of her own ready-made meals, each one neatly labelled.

The hunger that had nagged him all the way home now overwhelmed him. He closed the freezer door, opened the bread bin – also stocked full – and pulled out some rolls. The pantry, unsurprisingly, was also full of provisions. He took a jar of honey and was soon eating voraciously.

When he had finished, he walked upstairs to his room and found the things he needed, then left the house by the back door and made his way into Ashingford.

His entry to the squash club felt unreal. He had been prepared to parry questions but in the end he found the reception area unmanned and was able to slip in unnoticed and walk straight to the changing room.

There was no one there. He changed quickly, then walked with his rackets into the loo area and locked himself in one of the cubicles. He looked at his watch.

Nine o'clock. There would be some time to wait. He sat there, thinking of Abby. And as he thought of her and what had happened to her, he found the anger boiling up again.

Gradually people started to enter the changing room. He heard them talking and laughing, and recognized most of the voices. But he stayed where he was, his anger still bubbling as he focused his mind on the objects of his rage, and what he had come to do.

More people entered the changing room. He heard Andy speaking, and Joe, then more voices, and finally the two he had been listening for.

He stiffened. They were here at last. Only a few feet from him. He listened, clenching his fists.They talked for a while, loudly, con-

▷ **6** *eerie* ['ɪəri]: strange, mysterious and frightening **7** *immaculate:* extremely clean and tidy **12** *fastidious:* very careful that every detail is correct **17** *tough* [tʌf]: (here) difficult **31** *labelled:* beschriftet **32** *nag sb.:* (here) be in sb.'s mind continually **34** *pantry:* cupboard, closet or small room in a house used for storing food **40** *parry sth.:* etwas abwehren **44** *cubicle:* (hier) Einzeltoilette **48** *boil up:* (here) grow bigger and more dangerous **51** *bubble* (v): (here) (of a feeling) continue to be strong

fidently, then came into the loo and finally left. Others followed and soon the changing room was silent again.

Jamie looked at his watch and stood up.

The regional Championships were ready to start.

He unlocked the cubicle, walked out of the changing room and straight over to the tournament registration desk. Faces turned his way and he heard his name muttered all around him. But he took no notice. Brent Marrick was behind the desk.

'Jamie, what the –?'

'What court am I on?'

'Jamie, I thought … we all thought …'

'What court?'

'Court four. But look, is everything –?'

But Jamie turned away, ignoring all glances and attempts to speak to him, and made his way down to the courts.

There was no one on court four, and no one looking down from the gallery; but that was no surprise. Everyone would have been expecting a bye for Danny in the first round.

Jamie wasn't bothered. He no longer cared what anyone thought, except Abby, and this was for her. He did some stretching exercises, then started to hit the ball against the wall.

'Jamie!' A voice called down from the gallery.

He stopped and looked up to see Andy staring down at him.

'Jamie, I thought you … I mean –'

'I'm here,' Jamie said flatly. He meant no unpleasantness to Andy, no more than he had done to Brent, but right now he was not disposed to be sociable to anyone. He thought for a moment, then, feeling he had to offer Andy something, said: 'Good luck in the tournament.'

He paused, then added: 'I hope you win it.'

And he turned back to the front wall and started driving the ball against it again. Soon he heard more voices in the gallery. He did not turn round – he decided he would not turn round again – but he could hear it filling up rapidly, and people gabbling excitedly at the strange reappearance of someone they perhaps had thought dead.

He resolutely ignored them, even Joe who called down to ask where he'd been hiding himself. He kept his eyes on the little ball thudding down against the front wall and drove all his hatred into that.

The noise in the gallery was swelling to huge proportions. More voices called down to him, some joking, others serious, then a strange silence fell, as though the watchers had suddenly realized he was not going to turn and explain to them what had happened, was not going to acknowledge them; or perhaps they had simply been quelled by the strange, focused anger he felt as he struck the little ball, and thought of Abby, and how she had cried in his arms.

In that silence, he heard the door of the court open and shut. He turned and saw Danny walk forward. They looked at each other and the cockiness that he usually saw in the other boy was absent. In its place was confusion.

Danny held out another ball.

'The match ball. Joe just gave it to me.'

Jamie said nothing and merely took the ball, put his own in his pocket, and started to hit the new ball against the wall. Danny, looking somewhat edgy, took up his position on the other side of the court, and they went through the knock-up, neither speaking.

Above them, Jamie heard more voices, and now he spared a brief glance up there. It was crowded to capacity. He didn't suppose anyone was watching any of the other games. And for once – for the only time he could remember – his own father was not there.

He let his gaze rest on Bob Powell and made sure as their eyes met that the man caught every drop of the hatred intended for him.

'Change sides,' called the marker.

They changed sides and he practised on the backhand. It felt strange to be holding a racket again after so many days; more days without practice than he could ever remember. He had no plan, no tactics, no concern for himself. He was not playing for himself. He was not playing for his father.

He was playing for Abby.

And the mere sight of Danny and Bob Powell was making him angrier by the second.

'Spin, please,' called the marker.

▷ **26** *disposed:* willing or prepared · *be sociable:* enjoy spending time with other people **33** *gabble* (infml): talk quickly **43** *acknowledge sb.* [ək'nɒlɪdʒ]: show that you have noticed sb. · *quell sth.:* stop or reduce sth. (esp. strong feelings) **54** *edgy* (infml): nervous **69** *the mere sight of sb.:* der bloße Anblick von jdm.

Danny came over, still watching warily as though he found Jamie's manner unnerving. Jamie did nothing to make him feel better and simply stared back. Danny spun his racket and Jamie called.

'My serve,' said Danny, holding out the racket to show him.

But Jamie ignored him and simply turned to the backhand side of the court to receive serve. A hush fell over the gallery.

'Danny to serve,' said the marker. 'Love – all. Play.'

And the first serve came at him. He drove it back hard, far harder than he normally hit the ball, and harder than he needed to hit the ball. But the strange focus he felt, and the anger, and the communion he sensed with Abby, all seemed to favour him. He knew from that first shot that today was to be different.

He drove Danny to the back of the court and set up a series of drives that sent the boy scuttling from one side to the other. A few strokes later, he had regained the serve and never lost it again in that game.

'One – love.'

'Two – love.'

'Three – love.'

And so it went on, as he played like a man possessed. He had only one shot today, the lashing drive that sent Danny chasing from one corner to the other. Even at the front of the court he found he could not play a drop shot. His anger was too great; all he could do was drive the ball hard towards the nicks.

Usually for a winner.

When it wasn't a winner, his energy and his rage were so great that he was more than able to retrieve whatever Danny threw at him in return. Between points he saw the panic on the other boy's face. Danny's game was usually pacy. His own game was the more pedestrian. But the aggression Andy had told him he needed had come of its own volition. It would probably never come again.

'Nine – love. Game to Jamie.'

He turned without a word and walked off the court to fetch the towel from his bag. He heard murmurs up in the gallery, but shut his mind to them. He didn't care about their excitement. He didn't care about Danny's confusion. He didn't care about Bob Powell's shouts of exhortation, which had started towards the end of the last game once it became evident that Danny was being run off his feet.

Danny came off court, too, reached for his own towel and mopped his face.

'You're playing well,' he said, self-consciously.

Jamie stood up and stared at him; then, without a word, walked back on court, took the ball and started driving it against the wall again.

'Ease up on the ball, Jamie,' someone shouted up in the gallery. 'It's got to last for the rest of the match.'

He heard laughter from above, the kind of laughter that is a release from tension, but when he simply continued driving the ball without a backward glance or any response at all, the laughter fell away and the murmuring returned.

The door closed again and he saw Danny take up his position to receive serve. The boy's face looked pinched. He hadn't scored a point yet and he must be worrying not just about losing the match but being given the ultimate disgrace of a twenty-seven – love white-wash. Perhaps there would be tantrums in this game. There usually were.

Jamie shrugged. It would make no difference now.

'One game to love to Jamie,' called the marker.

'Love – all.'

He served, again a hard driving serve, and the pattern of the game continued. He drove and drove. When the ball came hard at him, he drove it hard back. When it came high, he smashed. When it was short to the front, he drove it hard down the line, or across court, or into the nicks.

All the shots he usually played, the lobs and boasts and drops, were gone today. He knew he could not play them. He had only anger. Sooner or later, he supposed, it would wear out, but he knew it was deep enough for what he had to do today.

▷ **10** *communion with sb.:* feeling of togetherness with sb. **14** *scuttle:* run with short steps **20** *possessed* [pəˈzest]: controlled by a spirit **21** *lashing:* peitschend **27** *retrieve sth.:* bring or get sth. back **29** *pacy* (infml): (here) quick and exciting **30** *pedestrian:* without any imagination or excitement, dull **31** *of its own volition:* by itself **37** *exhortation:* act of urging sb. on **47** *release* (n): act of freeing oneself from sth. **52** *pinched:* pale and thin because of worry **54** *disgrace:* shame **54–55** *whitewash* (infml): complete defeat in a sports game **55** *tantrum:* sudden, short period of angry unreasonable behaviour **67** *wear out:* (here) become less

It was not supposed to win matches. By all standards of logic, he knew he should not be playing as well as this. He was out of his mind with anger and, as the game progressed, he found that – far from subsiding – it was growing deeper. He was so incensed when Danny finally won his first point, that he smashed his backhand return of serve straight into the nick for an outright winner to regain the serve, then won the remaining three points of the game in a breathless succession of nicks and kills that sent the gallery into mad applause.

'Game to Jamie, nine – one,' he heard the marker say, as he walked off court again.

Now, as he towelled his face outside the court, he heard the noise in the gallery rising to a roar. Danny came off court, scowling, and this time avoided all attempts at small talk.

Jamie didn't bother glancing at him. Yet strangely, even in his fury, he was starting to feel a curious sympathy for Danny. He knew now that Danny was no more than the creation of another man's will. Something he himself might have been.

He turned back to the court, picked up the ball and, once again, started to pound it against the wall. A moment later he heard the door of the court close once more, as Danny entered. And this time, as he turned to look at his opponent, he caught a new face up in the gallery.

Dad.

So someone had contacted him. Brent probably or Joe. He turned and struck the ball hard against the wall again. It didn't matter. He had expected this. And nothing would change what he had come here to do.

'Jamie leads two games to love,' called the marker. 'Love – all.'

Silence fell once more. He glanced at Danny and saw his face etched with tension. Then he served, hard as usual, the only shot he knew today. Danny powered it back and the rally started. This time Jamie felt the desperate energy of his opponent. He knew Danny would throw everything he could into this game to try and salvage the match.

But the match was beyond salvage. Jamie knew it and he sensed, after he had weathered the onslaught, that Danny felt it too. Today was going to be his. He had summoned a whirlwind that would probably never visit him again. And somehow he hoped it would not. It was starting to frighten him.

At five – love ahead, he felt Danny's spirit drop. Up in the gallery he heard Powell bellowing encouragement. There was tension in that voice, too, just as there was in Danny's face; tension, embarrassment, even a touch of fear. To lose was one thing; to be annihilated was another.

And this was annihilation.

He heard the cheers, too, the cheers that had resounded throughout the match, yet they had been oddly muted cheers, as though everyone had been touched by the strangeness of this experience. 'Hand out. Love – Seven.'

So Danny was making a last-ditch fight and had regained the serve for the first time in ages. Jamie stared across at his opponent and almost snarled at him. It was so easy to summon the energy he needed: he only had to think of Abby, and Powell up there blustering in the gallery; and this boy here.

He drove the return of serve down the line. Danny raced after it and tried to play a cross-court, but it was a tired shot and Jamie barely needed to move to cut it off and smash it into the nick.

'Hand out. Seven – love.'

He took the ball and decided to serve from the lefthand box. Up in the gallery he sensed the tension mounting, even as it was down on court. No one spoke. He felt the eyes of everyone upon him. He stared at the little ball, then served, hard to the forehand.

Danny struck back, this time aiming down the line, and the ball clipped the top of the tin. Another tired shot. There was a gasp from the gallery.

Jamie picked up the ball and walked across to the right-hand service box.

'Eight – love,' called the marker. 'Game and match ball.'

He glanced at Danny. The boy was finished. The job was done. He made to serve hard as usual, then checked himself and played a lob serve. The only lob he had played in the whole match.

▷ **4** *subside:* grow weaker · *incensed:* angry **12** *scowl* [skaʊl]: look at sb. in an angry or annoyed way **29** *etched with sth.:* (here) clearly showing sth. **32** *salvage sth.:* manage to rescue sth. from a difficult situation **35** *weather sth.:* come safely through sth. (e.g. a difficult period or experience) · *onslaught* ['ɒnslɔːt]: strong, violent attack **36** *summon sth.:* make sth. come to you · *whirlwind:* (here) strong force **42** *annihilate sb.* [ə'naɪəleɪt]: destroy sb. completely **45** *resound* [rɪ'zaʊnd]: fill a place with sound **46** *muted:* quiet, not as loud as usual **49** *last-ditch:* final but useless **52** *bluster:* talk in an aggressive, threatening way, but with little effect

The ball climbed high, so high he feared it would come down out of court, but it fell just inside the red line and dropped beyond Danny's racket into the nick at the back of the court.

Jamie's mind raced back to the last shot of the last game they had played; and it seemed an appropriate irony that this match, too, should end on an ace.

'Game and match to Jamie, nine – love, nine – one, nine – love.'

Cheering and clapping broke out in the gallery. Jamie shook Danny briefly by the hand and strode away from the court without a word, leaving his rackets and bag behind. He had one more thing to do and he was going to do it now.

He ran up to the gallery. They cheered as he entered and hands clapped him on the back. Dad walked towards him.

But Jamie pushed straight past him.

'Bob, look out!' someone shouted.

Powell ducked, seeing what was coming, but he was not quick enough. Jamie threw himself on him, wrestled him to the ground and rained blows upon his face.

'Stop him!' Joe shouted.

Jamie felt hands seize him from all sides and drag him, struggling, from on top of Powell. Powell rolled to the side, wiping blood from his nose.

'What the ... bloody hell are you playing at?'

Jamie still fought to get at him but several people were holding him now. Then Dad stepped forward.

'Let him go. I'll take care of this.' He turned to Powell. 'I'm terribly sorry. I'll – '

'He'll pay for that.' Powell glared at Dad. 'You'll pay for that. I'll make sure your boy never –'

But Jamie didn't wait to hear the rest. He broke free and ran for the changing room, people stepping aside to let him pass. Behind him he heard a confusion of voices.

He stormed into the changing room. It was empty but he knew it would not be for long. He turned and waited, still bristling with anger. Then Dad stepped in.

They stared at each other in silence for a moment, then his father stepped forward.

Jamie pointed a finger at him and snarled, 'If you hit me once, I'll walk out of your life forever.'

Dad stopped. Then started forward again.

'I mean it!' snapped Jamie.

Dad stopped a second time, and they stared at each other again in silence. And now, as Jamie studied his father's face, he saw that it was unshaven, and seemed old and tired and sad.

But that was still not enough to quench his defiance.

'I'm only staying if you're going to be a proper father, and I'm giving up squash for a while. Maybe for ever. It'll be my decision.' He clenched his fists. 'I can live at home or I can live somewhere else. I don't have to stay at home but I'm telling you, if you try and push me around any more, or if you hit me or anything, then I'm off. For good.'

Dad watched him for a moment, his face dark and still. Then he looked down.

'Your mother's dead, Jamie.'

▷ **16** *duck* (v): move your head or body down to avoid being hit **18** *rain sth. down on sb.:* fall or make sth. fall on sb. in large quantities **34** *bristle with sth.:* contain a lot of sth. **45** *quench sth.:* (here) stop sth. **50** *for good:* permanently

TWENTY SIX

Jamie sat alone in the car in the squash club car park. He was still in his kit, his anger now spent, and he was filled with a sick confusion. After a while Dad appeared at the door of the club, carrying the squash bag he had left behind, and walked towards him.

Gone was the confident stride. This was an old man's walk. His father opened the door, climbed in and pulled the door to. They sat in silence for a moment.

'What happened?' Jamie said.

His father stared at the windscreen.

'I don't know if I've sorted it with Powell.' The voice was jaded, almost empty of expression. 'I've pulled you out of the tournament, obviously. They'd have disqualified you anyway. I apologized to Powell, said you'd been through a tough time. I don't know if he's going to press charges but Joe's calmed him down a bit.'

He frowned.

'I phoned the police while I was in there, told them you'd been found. They may want to come round and speak to you.'

Jamie said nothing. His question had not been about Powell or the tournament or the police, but Dad answered it now.

'She thought she was never going to see you again after she read your note. She rounded on me, accused me of destroying you, taking you away from her. Then she went into her shell and never came out of it again. Wouldn't look at me, wouldn't speak to me. It was like living with a mute. She spent every minute of the day busy round the house. I couldn't stop her. She was manic. She cleaned everything, made up stacks of meals and shoved them in the freezer, sent off the last of the Christmas cards.' He shook his head. 'The house is spotless now. Spotless and empty. But I guess you saw that when you collected your kit.'

Jamie bit his lip, unable to speak. Dad went on.

'Then yesterday she went to the hairdresser in the morning and came back and cooked me my lunch, and washed up all the things, and dried them and put them away. She wouldn't leave anything in the rack. Every single thing had to be put away.' He took a slow breath. 'I had to go out in the afternoon. When I got back, I found her lying on the bed. She'd made herself up, put on her best dress, and taken an overdose.' He looked down. 'There was nothing I could do.'

Jamie gripped the edge of the seat, too stunned to speak. Dad took another slow breath.

'They took the body away yesterday and I've ... I've been walking ever since. I just ... walked all night. I don't know where I've been. I only got back about ten and then Joe rang to say you were here.' Dad stopped, breathing hard, then reached across to the glove compartment and took something out. 'I found this on the bed beside her.'

Jamie stared.

It was his secret book.

He screwed up his eyes, racked with guilt at the thought that he had come home just a few hours too late. He could picture it all now. Mum must have found his book before he ran away. No wonder she'd been acting strangely. If only she'd confronted him about it. And then after he'd gone ...

All the cleaning and tidying and cooking and shopping. It was the way Mum would have acted. Making sure the house was as right as it could be – before taking herself off to die.

He heard his father crying and looked across. This was something he had never seen before. He felt his own tears start but checked them, somehow. There had to be something he could say. They both needed help now.

'Dad,' he said. 'Dad, listen ...'

His father stared at him, his face warped with grief.

'Dad, we'll ... pull through this somehow.'

▷ **10** *jaded:* tired and bored **14** *press charges:* officially accuse sb. of a crime **21** *round on sb.:* criticise or attack sb. **60** *warped:* twisted · *grief:* great sadness

His father still stared at him, his eyes so wild that Jamie thought for a moment he had not been heard. Then Dad reached out and put a hand on his shoulder.

And that was all.

Late in the afternoon he walked with Spider down to the playing fields at the end of the road.

His friend already knew about Mum.

'Christ, Jamie, I'm so sorry. I don't know what to say.'

Jamie looked down. 'Who told you about it?' he said. Though he didn't really care.

'Mrs Sanderson down the road. Don't know how she got to hear of it.'

Jamie frowned. If Mrs Sanderson knew about it, half of Ashingford would have heard about it by now. He shrugged. People had to find out some time.

'When's the funeral?' said Spider.

'Don't know yet. Dad's fixing it.'

They stopped by the swings in the children's playground and Spider spoke again.

'So what did you tell your dad about where you've been? And where have you been, by the way? If you don't mind my asking.'

Jamie thought back to Abby and all that had happened. Dad had not asked for explanations. No doubt he would later, as Spider was doing now.

But Jamie had already decided that he would never tell anyone about Abby, not even Spider. Abby was his own secret, the one part of his life he was proud of, and he wanted to keep it that way. Besides, she deserved as much privacy as possible if she was to start a new life for herself.

He reached out to the nearest swing and pushed it gently.

'I just drifted for a few days. Dossed about, got cold, hungry, came home again.'

'What about your mate?'

'Eh?'

'Your mate. The one I gave you the money for. Did you get him out of trouble?'

Jamie thought of Abby again, her beautiful face, her beautiful body, her mystery; the way she had needed him, for that short time.

'Yes,' he said, still seeing her in his mind. 'I got him out of trouble. He's OK now.'

'Good. Did you hear about those men? The ones who asked us about that girl they were looking for?'

Jamie pushed the swing again and tried not to sound interested.

'What about them?'

'The taller one's been stabbed to death and the other one's charged with his murder. There was a thing about it on the news.'

Jamie said nothing.

'It was a bit gruesome,' Spider went on. 'Apparently they were brothers and people saw a car pulled over at the side of the motorway with both doors open and these two fighting by the verge. There were lots of witnesses. The big guy was seen running away with blood streaming down his face, and the smaller guy caught him up and started stabbing him. Some men in a van pulled over and went to help but it was too late. Just as well we didn't bump into them again.'

Jamie looked away. So Angelo was dead. No doubt he'd told Vittorio the boy hadn't delivered the money so he could keep it for himself, and his brother hadn't believed him. It didn't matter now. What mattered was that they weren't going to bother Abby again.

Spider went on.

'I got loads of questions while you were away. It was bad enough with the police and Mum and Dad and half the street, but everybody at school was pumping me about you as well. Teachers, pupils, dinner ladies. Old Man Talbot had me in his office. Wanted to know if I'd seen you.'

'What did you tell him?'

'I told him what I said to everybody. I hadn't seen you and I didn't know where you were. The hardest questions were the ones about your state of mind.'

'Eh?'

'Some of them asked me if I thought you were depressed or suicidal or anything.'

'What did you say?'

▷ **16** *funeral:* ceremony for burying a dead person **45** *stab sb.:* push a knife into sb. to kill or injure them **48** *gruesome:* unpleasant, horrible **62** *pump sb.* (infml): try to get information from sb. by asking them lots of questions **62–63** *dinner lady:* woman who serves school lunches to students

'It was difficult. I mean, I've always said you were off your trolley anyway.' Spider checked himself. 'Sorry, mate. It's not the right time for jokes, is it?'

Jamie looked down.

'It's OK, but ... you'll have to be patient with me.'

Spider put an arm round him.

'I told them you'd seemed a little worried lately. That was the truth. I said I didn't know the reason. That wasn't. But I told them you had a squash tournament coming up and maybe that was part of it. I didn't give anything away. I hope I did the right thing.'

Jamie looked up again. He couldn't manage a smile but he did his best.

'You did all the right things. Thanks. You've been the best friend I could ever have had.'

He pulled the swing to him and sat on it.

'Careful,' said Spider. 'You're a bit big for that now. You're not a kid any more.'

Jamie gripped the chains and stared up at the grey sky.

No, he wasn't a kid any more. Indeed, it seemed to him now that he had suddenly grown very old. He wondered whether he would ever be able to grow young again.

TWENTY SEVEN

He found his father in the sitting room, in the chair Mum used to like. There was no light on and at first Jamie thought the room was empty; then he saw the figure sitting there, caught in the light from the hall.

He walked in and Dad turned to look at him. They faced each other in silence, not a hostile silence, but a silence in which Jamie felt they were each struggling to master a new language; a language they would have to learn quickly if they were to have a future together.

He knew his father was broken, just as he, too, was broken. Somehow, they had to build something on the ruins of what was left. Much that was bad seemed to have gone.

But the price had been terrible.

Dad stirred. 'Do you want something to eat?'

Jamie shook his head. His father reached over and flicked on the side light, and Jamie stared at the face now illuminated before him.

It was full of pain.

'Sit down, Jamie.' The voice was weary. It did not command; it did not hector. It almost asked permission. Jamie sat down in the chair opposite; and Dad went on, in the same tired voice.

'I don't really know where we go from here. You're mixed up. I'm mixed up. I've ...' He frowned. 'I've read what you said about me. I ... I suppose I must deserve it. I've always wanted the best for you. I've ... tried to give you the advantages I never had and push you, and ...' He stopped again, and his eyes slanted away towards the far wall.

▷ **1** *off your trolley* (sl): crazy, stupid **38** *hector sb.:* try to make sb. do sth. by talking or behaving in an aggressive way **44** *slant:* move downwards

Jamie watched, helplessly. And he realized suddenly that this man before him, now skewered with sorrow, was a man he had never known before; a man who had never known him; and who only now, it seemed, was starting to know himself.

He thought back to the man he had once feared.

But that man was gone.

Dad spoke again. 'I meant the best, Jamie. I meant the best but I've … I've made mistakes. And, my God, they've cost me dear.'

Jamie saw tears in Dad's eyes again and made to get up, but his father waved him back.

'Don't. I'll be all right. I'm more concerned about … getting you right again. I'm a fighter. I'll always pull through somehow. But –'

'I'm a fighter, too, Dad,' said Jamie, looking hard at him.

His father's face softened for a moment.

'Yes, Jamie. I know you are.' Dad leaned back in the chair, breathing slowly. 'Can you tell me where you went?'

Jamie looked away and Dad quickly spoke again.

'You don't have to tell me. I'm not going to push you. Just as long as you didn't get into any trouble.'

Jamie thought for a moment, then made up his mind.

'I ran away because I was mixed up about you, and Mum, and myself. But I also …' He hesitated. 'I also had to borrow some money, a hell of a lot of money. For a good cause, I promise you. Don't ask me what it was for because I'll never tell you.' He bit his lip, anxious not to compromise Spider. 'So I … borrowed it from a friend of mine who gave up all his savings to help me.'

'Spider.'

Jamie frowned, desperate not to put his friend in trouble. Dad spoke again.

'It's all right. I won't tell anybody. I won't tell him or his parents that I know. If he helped you like that, and it was for a good cause, like you say, then I admire him for it. I've obviously been wrong about him, like I have about everything else. How much do you owe him?'

'I'm … too embarrassed to say. It's such a lot of money. Several thousand.'

'Well, whatever it is, I'll give you the money and you can pay him back. You don't have to tell him it came from me. Leave it a few weeks, then tell him you inherited it or something or …' But Dad stopped again. Self-control was deserting him again. He clenched his fists over the arm of the chair. 'I'm sorry, Jamie, I seem to have done so much wrong. I just ... hope I can put some of it right.'

His body started to shake. Jamie hesitated, then stood up and walked over.

And this time his father did not wave him back.

In the night, he tossed in his bed, his mind wakeful with grief. Yet even in misery there seemed to be some kind of hope. His father had embraced him, said he was sorry, shown his own vulnerability, for the first time ever.

Perhaps it would never happen again. The fighter who had won all those squash tournaments in Australia back in the old days would surely set himself to the task of starting life all over again.

He did not know whether they had a future. He hoped so. But healing, if it came, would take time. Perhaps a whole life. As for himself ...

He had to start again, too.

He rolled over, thinking of Mum, and how peaceful her face had looked when Dad had taken him to the undertaker's. His own tears had started then, and he was glad. He needed to weep.

Somehow he fell asleep, but soon woke again. It was dark and the house was still, the street silent. The clock on the bedside table said half-past one.

And he found himself thinking of Abby.

On an impulse, he slid out of bed and dressed, then went downstairs and found the big lamp from the cupboard, and softly unlocked the back door, and walked out into the night.

The stars were out, it was a full moon, and there was a sharp chill in the air. He did not switch on the lamp, but walked to the gate, opened it as quietly as he could, and wandered down to the little shed where he had first seen the person who had changed his life.

He opened the door and looked in. There, in the corner, even without the lamp on, he could see the blankets they had used, and the

▷ **2** *skewered with sth.*: (here) feeling sth. throughout one's being **25** *compromise sb.* ['kɒmprəmaɪz]: say sth. about sb. that they do not want others to know about **45** *toss* (v): move from side to side **47** *vulnerability:* state of being weak and easily hurt **57** *undertaker:* person whose job it is to prepare dead people for burial **63** *on an impulse*: without really thinking

old cushion, and, after a moment, even the spare cup that went with the thermos flask. He must have left that behind.

He went over to the corner, tidied the blankets, and lay down, listening to the silence, and his own feverish breathing. Then he switched on the lamp and shone it against himself.

And there on the timbered wall close by, as though lying with him, was his shadow.

Abby's words came back to him.

'Whenever you see your shadow, Jamie, just remember you're looking at me.'

And in the silence of the night the shadow moved as he moved, and breathed as he breathed, and wept as he wept.

And then was gone.

THE GAME OF SQUASH

Squash court

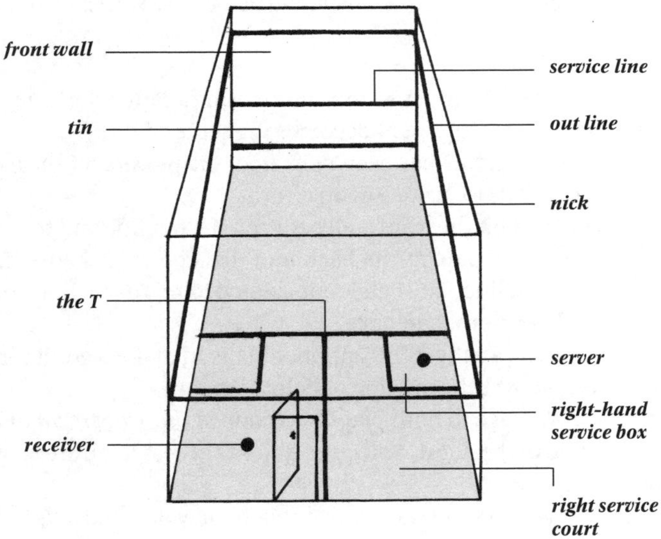

The rules of squash

Words found in *Shadows* are printed in italics and are underlined.

The warm up or knock up: Before the start of a match, the two players are allowed to 'warm-up' themselves and the ball on the match court.

The service: Play commences with a service. The person who serves first is decided by the *spin* of a racket. The player who does not spin the racket *calls out* which side he or she thinks the racket will land on. If he or she is correct, he or she is the server. The other player is the receiver.

The server must stand with at least part of one foot on the floor within the service box. For a service to be good, it is served directly onto the *front wall* above the service line and below the out line so that on its return it reaches the floor within the service court opposite the server's *service box*.

At the beginning of each game and when the service changes from one player to the other, the server can serve from either service box. After winning a *rally* (i.e. a series of hits and returns) the server then continues serving from the alternate box.

The player who wins the preceding game serves first in the next game.

Play: The server continues serving until losing a rally, when there is a '*hand out*', i.e. the opponent becomes the server.

After a good service has been delivered, the players hit the ball in turn until one fails to make a good return.

The ball must hit the front wall between the out line and the *tin* to be good. The ball may hit the back and the side walls between the *nick* and the out line. The ball is considered *dead* (or to die) when it has hit the floor more than once.

A player wins a rally if the opponent fails to make a good service or hits the ball over the out line or below the tin.

It is of advantage to both players to control *the T position* or area in the middle of the court, as it gives quicker access to all areas of the court.

If one player is in the way, the opponent may demand a '*let*'. A let is an undecided rally. The rally does not count and the server serves again from the same box.

Scoring: A *match* is the best of five *games*. Each game is played to nine *points*, unless the score reaches eight-all (i.e. both players have eight points). At eight-all the receiver has to choose to play either to nine points or to ten points.

Points are scored only by the server. When the server wins a rally, he or she scores a point; when the receiver wins a rally, he or she becomes the server.

The scoring is done by the *marker*.

Here are various terms from the novel used in scoring:

- *final game:* the fifth and last game in a match
- *a two-love lead:* one player has won two games and leads against his opponent, who has won no games ('love'); it can also refer to points in a game, e.g. 'two – love' means the server has

won two points and the receiver none and 'love – all' means no points have been scored so far.

- *game and match ball:* the state of the score when the server requires one point to win the game and the match.
- *penalty point:* point awarded against somebody; if the penalty point is against the server, the server gives the serve to the receiver; if the penalty point is against the receiver, the server gains a point.

Various types of shots

ace: a service shot which the receiver completely misses
backhand shot: a shot played in which the back of the hand holding the racket is turned towards the direction of the shot
forehand shot: a shot played in which the front of the hand holding the racket is turned towards the direction of the shot
bury the ball: cause the ball to die
curler/floater: a light service shot that goes high and comes down near the back of the court
volley: a shot in which the ball is returned before it bounces

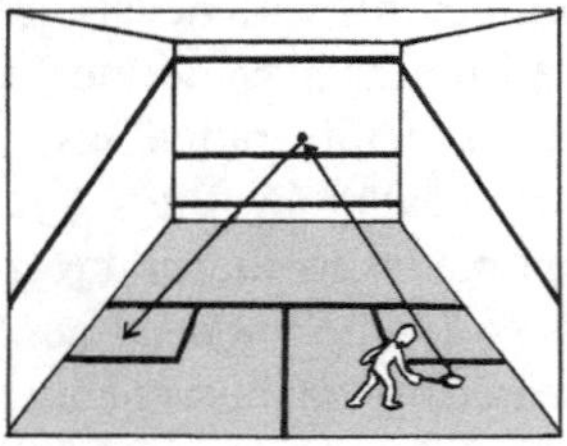

cross court

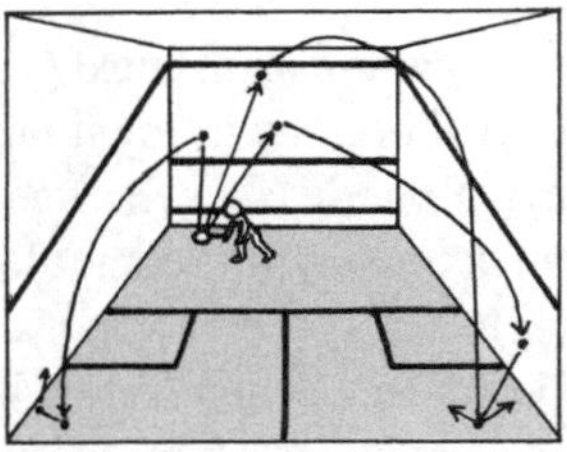

lobs

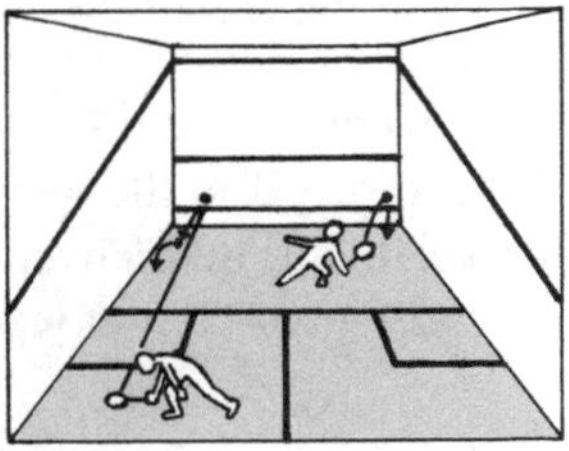

drop shots

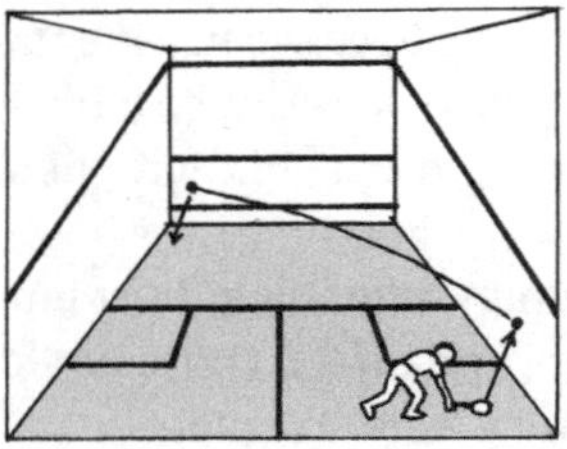

boast

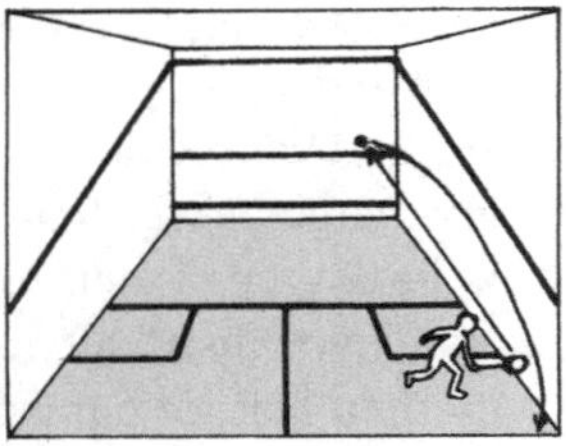

drive (also long line)

1

NEW YORK BELONGS TO WILLIAMS

Father exults as youngest daughter makes history

There is a madness in New York City. On a ravishingly clear and sunny late summer's day Serena Williams beat Martina Hingis 6-3, 7-6 on Saturday to become the first African-American woman since Althea Gibson in 1958 to win the US Open title, while just a few miles away 'mosquito-killing squads' were attempting to halt the spread of a killer disease, St Louis encephalitis.

Laconic New Yorkers here returned home after the women's final celebrations wondering if a little of Mayor Rudolph Giuliani's toxic spray should have been aimed at Serena's father, Richard, who in the wake of his younger daughter's magnificent victory – which she followed yesterday by winning the doubles title with her sister Venus with a 4-6, 6-1, 6-4 defeat of Chanda Rubin and Sandrine Testud – continued to poison the air with his idiosyncratic ramblings.

He suggested Lindsay Davenport, beaten by the 17-year-old Serena in the semi-finals, should be 'taken to the junkyard' and claimed that Hingis, still the world's No 1, who knocked out Venus in the other semi-final, 'had been so scared before she went out for the final that I told one doctor he should be standing by in case she had a heart attack'.

And so it went on. 'Venus will win two grand slams next year and is still the best player in the world. They'll both be in the finals next year; they've already taken over tennis. Nobody can sell sweets and popcorn like they can. Tennis was dead before my girls came along ...' And on.

Much is harmless, although two years ago, when Venus barged into Romania's Irina Spirlea during a changeover, he was quick to raise the race issue, calling Spirlea a 'big white turkey'. Williams is a complex man and it is not always possible to gauge his intent. As the years roll on, and Venus and Serena gain in maturity, he is likely to be increasingly marginalised, but for the present his self-publicity is feeding on the oxygen of their success. [...]

It was quickly realised, after a bumpy beginning, how much the sisters, with their flair for publicity on and off the court, could bring to the women's game and gradually they were accepted.

Of course, the playing rivalry between Hingis and the Sisters Sledgehammer has not gone away and never will. They want to get to the top; Hingis wants to stay there.

Richard Williams planned that Venus would reach the top first, and when she and Serena reached this year's Lipton championships final this year it was no surprise that Venus won. Their father then predicted the first 'all-black final' here, but Hingis won a stunning 6-1, 4-6, 6-3 semi-final over Venus on Friday night.

For Hingis, who ended the French Open in emotional turmoil after losing to the now retired Steffi Graf of Germany, and then bombed out of Wimbledon in the first round against the 16-year-old Australian Jelena Dokic, this last fortnight has seen her re-establish her credibility.

She is back with her mother and coach, Melanie, and has clearly worked extremely hard on her stamina, as she proved against Venus who ended their match badly cramped and virtually unable to serve. But two Williamses was too much for Hingis in this ridiculously scheduled, television-driven tournament with its back-to-back semis and finals. [...]

This was not a great final, for the huge battle with Venus had taken the physical and mental edge off Hingis. Serena raced to a 3-0 first-set lead, then her nerves began to grip. She survived two break points before serving out the first set, and missed two match points at 5-3 in the second set before, half an hour later, decisively winning the tie-break 7-4.

▷ **2** *ravishing(ly):* extremely beautiful **5** *US Open:* important international tennis championship **6** *squad:* (hier) Truppe **7** *St.Louis encephalitis:* Hirnhautentzündung **8** *laconic:* (here): not using many words **10–11** *in the wake of sth.:* following sth. **14** *idiosyncratic:* unusual and eccentric · *ramblings:* long and confused speeches/interviews **21** *grand slam:* one of the four most important tournaments (US Open, Wimbledon, French Open, Australian Open) **26–27** *barge into sb.:* bang into sb. rudely **27** *changeover:* act of changing sides on the tennis court **29** *gauge sb.'s intent:* understand what sb. wants or means **31** *marginalise sb.:* make sb. less influential **55–56** *take the edge off sb.:* (here) make sb. weaker **57** *her nerves began to grip:* she began to get nervous · *break point:* (in tennis) situation in which if you lose the next point you lose the game in which you were serving **58** *serve out sth.:* (here) win sth. **59–60** *tie-break:* extra game in a set which decides who wins the set

'After I lost those two match points I was very upset with myself,' said Williams, who had won four three-setters in a row to reach the final. 'I said, "Serena, this can't happen. There comes a time when you have to stop caving, you just have to stop." You get so tired of going down because of the same problem. I just said to myself, "You're going to have to perform".'

The main difference between the two players was the power of the Williams serve, both first and second.

So Hingis missed her sixth grand slam title and Serena, who received the obligatory telephone call from President Clinton, won her first. As for her sister Venus, she has none. 'Venus was really down,' said Serena. 'I've never seen her that down before.'

It will now be fascinating to see what effect this victory has on all three women, as well as Davenport, the former US and reigning Wimbledon champion. Asked what she thought of Richard Williams predicting Venus would win two grand slams next year, Hingis, with a large grin, replied: 'What if I say "no comment"?'

Hingis and the Williams were dubbed the Spice girls of tennis, then the Spite girls. Just make that inspired.

▷ **2** *three-setter:* game consisting of three sets **4** *cave:* give in, lose

2

THE ONLY THING I COULD DO WAS RUN AWAY

'It's so cold on the streets and so frightening,' says Marie, a 20-year-old student who ran away from a Birmingham care home just before she was 16. She felt that she had no choice but to run away because the stepfather who had sexually abused her as a child, which led to her going into care in the first place, kept following her. He would appear and sit next to her as she sat on the bus to school, and hang around the care home.

'When I was 12 he was jailed for the abuse for a while, but it was all over the papers and everyone knew what he had done to me,' she says. 'In the end, I couldn't stand it and felt the only thing I could do was run away.'

She finished her GCSEs, took a job washing up in a restaurant for three weeks to save enough money for a train ticket to London, and then ran.

'The worst thing was that no one would listen to me,' she recalls. 'I was scared and nervous when I got on the train, but I felt I couldn't go back to the situation I had left behind. Kids will only run away if the situation they are in is so bad that living on the streets seems like a better option. Something has got to be really wrong to make a young person do a thing like that.'

Marie was so terrified when she arrived at Euston station that she simply walked the streets for three days – too frightened of what might happen if she lay down and closed her eyes. 'I felt so alone in the world,' she says. 'Nobody in my care home bothered to report me missing. The streets are full of homeless young people crying out for love.'

Marie was one of an estimated 129,000 young people who run away each year. The commonest reasons for children taking flight include desperation at not being listened to, rows with parents over

▷ **2** *care home:* Pflegeheim **4** *abuse sb.:* jdn. missbrauchen **5** *would:* (here) used to **12** *GCSE = General Certificate of Secondary Education:* a series of exams taken at the age of 16 **22** *Euston* ['juːstən]: large railway station in London **24** *bother to do sth.:* sich die Mühe machen, etwas zu tun **27** *an estimated …:* about …

the amount of freedom they are allowed, bullying at school, and drug problems or abuse at home.

[...] By the age of 16, one in nine children will have run away for at least one night, with a quarter of those ending up sleeping rough. Some have to survive through begging, stealing or prostitution, and many are sexually abused on the streets.

While children like Marie, who have been in care, make up a large proportion of runaways (approximately four in 10), the report finds that 21% are fleeing stepfamilies, and 13% one-parent families, compared to 7% who live with both birth parents. But, contrary to stereotype, poverty was found not to be a significant factor leading to young people running away: those from leafy suburbs are just as likely to flee as those from deprived inner-city areas. The majority of runaways are aged between 13 and 16 and are more likely to be girls than boys (although boys tend to run away earlier and more often). It is not only a problem of troubled adolescence: an estimated 18,000 children under 11 also run away each year, of whom about a third are under eight. Shockingly, a further 18,000 children a year are thrown out by their parents. The report also notes that the longer runaways are away, the more vulnerable they become.

There is no national network of services in place, so emergency organisations like Childline find it very hard to refer children who phone in a crisis to appropriate local services. The report proposes a series of measures both to prevent young people from running away in the first place, and to provide decent support services when they do.

Plans include an interview for each young person who has run away to identify the reasons for fleeing, and to try to tackle them rather than just dumping the children back in the situation from which they have fled; a network of refuges so that young people are not forced to live rough; and the establishment of a named person in each area to co-ordinate services for runaways.

Chris, now 20, ran away from numerous care placements about 20 times. He believes that refuges are essential, but also that fundamental changes in the care system are necessary. [...]

The government has highlighted a small project in Gloucester called Astra (Alternative Solutions to Running Away), which employs just three part-time workers, as a model of good practice. The project works with young people who have run away to prevent recurrences. Staff listen to young people's concerns and then try to work with them, their parents and other agencies (such as schools and social services) to find solutions with which both the young people and their parents or carers are happy. Police estimate that the project has reduced the number of repeat runaways by 61%.

One former runaway, Sally, 14, says the project has helped her resolve a difficult situation with her mother: 'My mum didn't like my friends, the way I dressed or the fact that I wore make-up, and she didn't like me going out. One day, I just didn't go home from school. I was scared because I didn't know where I could go. In the end, I stayed at a friend's house. Astra talked to my mum and talked to me. Now she gives me a bit more freedom, I understand her better and she understands me better.'

Now that Marie is settled in London, studying for a university degree and living in a flat that a Children's Society-supported tenancy project helped to secure for her, the days of trudging around the capital's West End with nowhere to go seem very far off.

'I love my home,' she says. 'I've got my own front room, my own bedroom, a cat, friends and a normal life. I don't ever want to go through what I went through again. And if young people like me had more rights, they wouldn't have to either.'

▷ **12** *leafy suburbs:* areas where people live in nice houses with gardens **13** *deprived:* underprivileged, poor **24** *measure:* Maßnahme **28** *tackle sth.:* deal with sth. **33** *care placement:* (hier) Plegeheim/-familie **36** *Gloucester* ['glɒstə]: town in west England **40** *recurrence:* act of happening again · *staff:* people who work in an institution (e.g. school) **54–55** *tenancy project:* Wohnprojekt **55** *trudge around:* (here) walk and hang around with nothing to do

THE AUTHOR

Tim Bowler was born in Leigh-on-Sea, Essex, in 1953, and studied Scandinavian literature at the University of East Anglia. He used to work as a foreign-language teacher in various schools before deciding to write full-time.

His first novel, *Midget* (1994), was well-received, but it was *River Boy* (1998) that brought him fame. It was awarded various prizes.

His other novels include *Dragon's Rock* (1995) and *Storm Catchers* (2001).